W9-BBD-627

BORODIN

THE COMPOSER & HIS MUSIC

AMS PRESS
NEW YORK

A. P. BORODIN

(By permission of M. P. Belaieff, St. Petersburg.)

Frontispiece

BORODIN

THE COMPOSER & HIS MUSIC

A DESCRIPTIVE AND CRITICAL ANALYSIS OF HIS WORKS
AND A STUDY OF HIS VALUE AS AN ART-FORCE

With many References to the Russian
Kouchka Circle of Five—Balakirev,
Moussorgsky, César Cui and Rimsky-
Korsakov with Borodin

By Gerald E. H. ABRAHAM

LIBRARY
SEMINOLE COMMUNITY COLLEGE

WITH PORTRAITS AND MUSICAL EXAMPLES

REC. MAY 2 2 1978

SANFORD, FLORIDA
32771

WILLIAM REEVES
Bookseller Limited.

83 Charing Cross Road,
— London W.C.2. —

Library of Congress Cataloging in Publication Data

Abraham, Gerald Ernest Heal, 1904-
    Borodin, the composer & his music.

    "With many references to the Russian Kouchka (circle
of five): Balakirev, Moussorgsky, César Cui, and Rimsky-
Korsakov with Borodin."
    Reprint of the 1927 ed. published by W. Reeves,
London.
    1. Borodin, Aleksandr Porfir'evich, 1833-1887.
ML410.B73A4   1976   780'.92'4 [B]   74-27324
ISBN 0-404-12851-3

Reprinted from an original copy in the collections
of the Ohio State University Libraries

From the edition of 1927, London
First AMS edition published in 1976
Manufactured in the United States of America

AMS PRESS INC.
NEW YORK, N. Y.

FOREWORD.

I N this work it has been my object to describe, not everything that Borodin wrote, but those compositions only which are interesting, important or likely to be heard, and which may be regarded as *alive*. The discussion of mere student productions seems to me to be no more profitable than the narration of biographical facts which have no bearing on an artist's intellectual development. In the case of Borodin even this mental evolution, so obvious in the case of men like Beethoven and Wagner, is difficult to trace. His serious creative career, covering only twenty-five years (1862-1887), begins with a comparatively mature work, the First Symphony, and his numerous scientific and sociological activities rendered his musical productivity, even during that period, intermittent. As a consequence, any attempt to trace his evolution step by step is both unnecessary and impossible in a work of this limited scope.

In conclusion, I must confess my indebtedness to various sources for biographical and other data, and especially to M. Montagu-Nathan's "History of Russian Music," the same author's "Introduction to Russian Music," and various writings of Mrs. Rosa Newmarch

G. E. H. A.

CONTENTS.

LIST OF PORTRAITS.

BORODIN AS COMPOSER

I.—THE MAN AND THE TIME.

IT would be difficult to conceive of ideals
more noble and, apparently, more difficult of
attainment than those which animated a little
group of Russian musical amateurs in the
middle of the last century. To found a
national school of composition, deriving its
musical basis from the rich stores of national
folk-song and having as a literary source of
inspiration the fantastic fairy-tales of Slavonic folk-lore; to discover a form of music-
drama which should be melodious without
being Italian, and dramatically and logically
sound without being Wagnerian; and last,
but by no means least, to bring their work
before an indifferent, if not hostile, public,
and compel it to recognise its merit; such

was the truly Herculean task which the members of the "Invincible Band" set themselves—a task the more difficult in that they had but few satisfactory models to work from, little encouragement from the leading Russian musicians of the time, and in one or two cases a somewhat defective knowledge of the fundamental technique of musical composition.

Michael Glinka, who died in 1857, had been the first to turn his attention to the possibilities of purely Russian music, based on folk-song and the music of the Orthodox Church. His usual method was to use actual folk-tunes rather than to imitate them, or assimilate and reproduce their general feeling, but his treatment was so sympathetic and artistic as to serve as a tangible proof to his contemporaries of what could be done with such material. Indeed, in spite of foreign (chiefly Italian) influences in his work, which he was unable to eradicate, his work, while not greatly inspired, can still give more than a merely archæological pleasure.

His well-known orchestral fantasia, "Kamarinskaia," is the first instance of symphonic treatment being accorded to Russian peasant-tunes, and is hence the first of a line of works which includes such master-pieces as Rimsky-Korsakov's "Grande Pâque Russe." Folk-tunes, both Russian and Polish, are also used in Glinka's opera, "A Life for the Czar" (1836), a work which was, in a measure, the foundation-stone of Russian music. This was based on an incident in Russian history, and in his next operatic work, "Russlan and Ludmilla" (1842), Glinka drew for the first time upon the apparently inexhaustible store of Russian fairy-tales which Rimsky-Korsakov, Liadov, Balakirev, Stravinsky and others have since exploited so thoroughly. Meanwhile a younger man than Glinka, Alexander Dargomijsky, who had been dabbling in operatic composition of the conventional type, came under the former's influence and produced in 1856 a more artistic composition, "Russalka," based on a legendary theme and also follow-

ing Glinka's ideals in trying to throw off the
fetters of conventional Italian opera—in-
sipid plots, set-numbers, "prima-donna-
ism," debasement of the orchestra and
tawdriness in general. These ideals, in a
more developed state, were embodied in a
later work, a setting of Pushkin's drama,
"L'Hôte de Pierre," which, though comparatively unimportant from the point of view of
intrinsic value, became a sort of rallying-
point for all the operatic reformers of the
period in Russia—offering as it did an apparently safe passage between the Scylla of
Italianism and the Charybdis of Wagnerian
theories, either of which would have been
fatal to a truly "nationalist" style.

In "L'Hôte de Pierre" Dargomijsky more
or less abandoned "set-numbers" (i.e., isolated solos, duets and choruses) in favour of
a sort of continuous, lyrical recitative, which
was, however, unlike Wagner's in being more
melodic than declamatory. Hence there
was no necessity to bring the orchestra into
prominence to supply the purely musical in·

terest lacking in the vocal parts, while the leit-motif was relegated to its original office of heightening or creating dramatic effect, instead of being used as a vital part of the whole musical fabric. In so far that he wished to make music, words, action and scenery into a composite whole, in which none should predominate but each should be complementary of the rest, Dargomijsky was in accord with Wagner, but in every other respect his theories were perfectly free from Wagnerism.

Dargomijsky's operatic experiments and, still more, Glinka's essays in nationalism, had the effect of firing the imagination of an enthusiastic young man, who was personally acquainted with both the older men. This young man, Mily Alexeivich Balakirev, was a wealthy amateur (though with a sound technical equipment) and possessed of enormous powers of energy and organisation; not merely an enthusiast in himself, he possessed the vital power of creating enthusiasm in others, and in the years 1857-1862

gradually gathered around him the little
circle of dilettantes to whom I have alluded
in the beginning of this chapter.   None were
professional musicians (two were military
officers, one was a sailor, and the other a
medical student), but they were united by
common aims and by mutual admiration and
affection.   Naturally Glinka was their chief
model, but Dargomijsky's "Russalka"
seemed to them to be nearer their ideal of
lyric drama, and when, partly encouraged by
their interest, he produced "L'Hôte de
Pierre" they at once accepted it as a stan-
dard of method and theoretical excellence.
It must be understood, however, that the
"Five" did not bind themselves by cast-iron
rules or adhere blindly to pre-conceived
theories.   Each member was free to follow
his own line of advance, provided it was in
the common direction, and, though advice
was freely interchanged and collaboration
was almost as much the rule as the exception, the individual characteristics of each
member of the circle (known variously as the

"Five," the "Kouchka" and "The Invincible Band") remained perfectly distinct.

Balakirev—virtuoso of the piano—was the leader, the driving force and even to a considerable extent the teacher; extending the dominating influence of his dynamic personality not only over his immediate friends but even over the young Tchaïkovsky, who was then wavering between genuine nationalism and the Western eclecticism of his friends, the brothers Anton and Nicholas Rubinstein, who, as professional musicians, trained in the German traditions, scoffed at the empirical efforts of amateurs like those of the "Invincible Band."

César Cui, whose work as a composer is quite negligible and scarcely possesses any national flavour at all, was the propagandist member of the "Five," and waged furious and unceasing war on the very cosmopolitanism which he practised in his own music; his acid pen was, however, no mean auxiliary to a movement which was being obstructed both by aristocratic prejudice and academic ridicule.

Of the other three members of the group, Moussorgsky stands out as the grim realist, the daring harmonic innovator and the supreme genius of Russian opera, and Rimsky-Korsakov as the master of orchestration —perhaps the finest since Berlioz, and, like the Frenchman, author of a monumental treatise on the subject.   Regarding the fifth, Borodin, who is the subject of the present little book, it is far less easy to generalise, for his musical output, while entirely stamped by his own peculiar semi-Oriental individuality, is marked by no one character-istic which predominates to the detriment of the rest; it has many of the virtues of his friends' music without their failings—the "dryness" of Cui, the wild programmatic extravagances of Moussorgsky (which some-times, as in some of the well known "Tab-leaux d'une Exposition" result in sheer ugliness which no amount of cleverness can excuse) and the thematic weaknesses of Rimsky-Korsakov.   Borodin was the "all-round" man of the "Five" and his work is at once the most characteristically Russian, the soundest and the most beautiful of that produced by the group; in the matter of influence over later composers only Rimsky-Korsakov's has been as great, and that only in the sphere of the orchestra. The spirit which guides the direction of the most typically Russian music of to-day is derived immediately from Borodin.

Alexander Porphyrievich Borodin, the illegitimate son of a Georgian prince, was born on October 31, 1834, in that variously named city which was then known as St. Petersburg. He was brought up by his mother, who seems to have been a wise and liberal-minded woman, and at an early age began to show leanings towards the two subjects which between them divided practically the whole of his life-interest—science and music. He had already at nine years of age, tried his hand at composition, and at thirteen he produced a concerto for flute and piano (he having learned to play the former instrument). Another juvenile effort in the realm of chamber music was based on a theme from Meyerbeer's happily defunct "Robert le Diable," which, it is interesting to note, had previously served Chopin as a source of, rather doubtful, inspiration. But music was not to be his vocation; his mother wished that he should enter the medical profession and at the age of sixteen he was sent to the St. Petersburg Academy of Medicine. Here he remained for six years but, despite the fact that he never neglected his scientific work, still managed to hear, and even participate in the performance of, a great deal of music. His was no mere drawing-room devotion to the art, like Glinka's at a similar age, but a passion so genuine that to remedy his technical shortcomings he gave time to contrapuntal study beside exercises in free composition. Unlike Schumann, Borodin seems to have been able to reconcile himself to the interference of non-musical work with his artistic development, but it must be admitted that science was perfectly congenial to Borodin, while there was certainly nothing of the lawyer in Schumann.

In 1856, Borodin passed out of the academy and received an appointment in a military hospital. It was an important year in the composer's life, for in the autumn his military duties brought him into contact with Moussorgsky, then a seventeen-year old subaltern in Préobajensky regiment. They met on various occasions at the house of one of Borodin's superiors, and though their acquaintanceship did not deepen into real friendship till 1862, the younger man's outspoken remarks on the subject of nationalism turned Borodin's mind in that direction for the first time. Hitherto, owing to his environment he had only been brought in touch with the western classics and, indeed, he always retained a deep respect for Beethoven.

In 1858, Borodin graduated as a Doctor of Medicine, and in the years 1859-62, made an extensive European tour for scientific purposes—visiting Italy, Austria, Germany

and France. Musically, this tended naturally to re-establish the dominion of German
music in his mind for a time, a dominion
which required another meeting with the
enthusiastic Moussorgsky to shake it. A
more fortunate result was a meeting at Heid-
elberg, with the lady, Mdlle. Catherine
Protopova, who afterwards became his wife.

1862 was a most important landmark in
Borodin's career. He received a permanent
scientific appointment—that of assistant lec-
turer at the St. Petersburg Medical Academy—which allowed him time to devote to
his art. Meeting Moussorgsky again he was
introduced by him to Balakirev, the latter
being full of projects for his "Free School
of Music," founded in the capital to spread
the teachings of the nationalist school as a
counterbalance to the cosmopolitan aca-
demicism of the new official conservatoire
just set up under Anton Rubinstein. Borodin's conversion to nationalist aims now
became complete. He resumed the study of
composition, under Balakirev, and began to

work at his first serious composition, the Symphony in E flat, which took him five years to complete. The unusual length of time is easily accounted for. In 1863 he married Mdlle. Protopova, the lady being herself a musician, and the married life seems to have been quite idyllic. In the same year he commenced a series of lectures on chemical subjects at the School of Forestry and, in 1864, received the appointment of Professor of Organic Chemistry at the Military Academy, which he held till his death. Seeing that he was simultaneously engaged in propaganda for the emancipation of women (and more especially for their admission into the medical profession), as well as in the theoretical study under Balakirev, it is scarcely to be wondered at that his health suffered and the symphony made but slow progress.

This work received its first performance at St. Petersburg on January 4, 1869, at a concert of the Imperial Russian Musical Society directed by Balakirev, who was the society's conductor. ՙ Despite difficulties in rehearsal and the hostility of the academic party, one of whom, the well known critic, Alexander Serov, wrote that "a symphony by somebody named Borodin pleased only his friends, who, though few in number, applauded so insistently as to compel the composer to appear on the platform," the work was well received (the scherzo being encored) and when, later, it was performed in Germany the progressive elements in that country, of whom Liszt was the leader, were unstinting in their praise.

In the years 1869-72 Borodin was engaged in song writing and in work upon an opera, "La Fiancée du Tsar," based on a play by Meÿ, which Rimsky-Korsakov afterwards used as an operatic libretto. This, however, came to nothing and in 1871 was abandoned in favour of a new opera. Vladimir Stassov, the celebrated critic and a warm champion of the nationalist projects of "The Invincible Band," sketched out for him plans for a work on the subject of the historic legend

of "Prince Igor," but Borodin, after undertaking numerous researches to ensure historical accuracy in his treatment of the subject, abandoned it, in 1872, to start work on
a second symphony, which was not, however, completed for four years.

During this period he was simultaneously
engaged in organising his new Medical
School for Women, in heavy professional
duties at the Military Academy, in writing
several scientific works on the most abstruse
chemical subjects and in the composition of
part of an opera-ballet, "Mlada," which was
never performed and on which he again lav-
ished an enormous amount of trouble in
historical and archæological research alone.
Having completed the finale of "Mlada,"
he returned to "Prince Igor" (which he
never finished entirely) and continued to
work also at the Second Symphony which
was completed late in 1876, and received its
première at St. Petersburg in February of
the next year, under the baton of E. F.
Napravnik, who, as a member of the eclectic

party, was scarcely the most sympathetic interpreter. It is not surprising that, under such circumstances, its success was only moderate. Its real vogue dates from the 1879 performance under Rimsky-Korsakov, in a slightly revised form. It is now considered, indisputably, to be not only Borodin's masterpiece, but one of the finest symphonic works of the nineteenth century.

In 1877 Borodin paid his second visit to Germany—partly for scientific purposes, but more particularly to meet the veteran Liszt, the untiring champion of all artistic progressivism of whatever school, who wrote more bad music and helped more good than any other man in the nineteenth century. He welcomed Borodin whole-heartedly to Weimar and gave him every encouragement, and Borodin seems to have fully reciprocated his admiration. He appears to have been forcibly struck by the Hungarian composer's resemblance to Balakirev, and, indeed, the two men had many points in common—for not only were both possessed of phenomenal powers as pianists, but each was an ardent advocate of musical nationalism and the possessor of a dominating, forceful personality which made him a natural leader of any intellectual movement in which he interested himself.

Borodin visited Germany again in 1881, having in the interval, worked again at "Prince Igor," written the well-known orchestral piece, "On the Steppes of Central Asia," which he dedicated to Liszt, and turned his attention, for the first time since his student efforts, to chamber-music.

Another Western tour, of a more extended nature, was made in 1885-6, when he visited Belgium in the company of César Cui, who had been invited to direct performances of his opera, "The Prisoner of the Caucasus," at Liége. The visit, which had been largely arranged by the Countess Mercy-Argentau, an admirer of the new Russian school, was a huge triumph for both composers, who conducted their own compositions with the greatest success in Brussels, Antwerp and other

large towns.   They were overwhelmed with
compliments, offers of engagements and
other tributes of esteem, and each returned
thanks to their friend the Countess by dedi-
cating to her a suite for piano—Cui, the
cycle, " À Argenteau," and Borodin, the well-
known " Petite Suite."   After the joy of this
sincere and wide-spread recognition came an
unfortunate reaction.   On his return to
Russia, Borodin found his wife, never in the
best of health, seriously ill at Moscow, and
his mother-in-law dying.   This extra strain
upon his own none too robust constitution
already sorely tried by the incessant trials to
which he had always subjected it, was too
much for it, and his friends experienced a
great shock when, immediately after his return to St. Petersburg, he died suddenly on
February 15, 1887—the immediate cause of
death, however, being the rupture of an ar-
tery.   His death was the second break in the
circle of the " Kouchka," Moussorgsky
having pre-deceased him by nearly six years,

and both composers were buried in the Alexander Nevsky Cemetery at St. Petersburg.

If, as Carlyle said, the only true happiness of a man is that of "clear, decided activity in the sphere for which, by nature and circumstances, he has been fitted and appointed," Alexander Borodin must have been a supremely happy man. And, despite his own and his wife's ill-health and the occasional fits of depression to which he (in common with almost all creative artists) was subject, there is no doubt that his life *was*, on the whole, a particularly happy one. Of a sympathetic and affectionate disposition, his love was extended not merely to individuals but to his fellow-men in the mass, and his one object in life was to show his sympathy in practical forms. It was his special good-fortune to be able to do this in two ways—by his medical and sociological work during his life and by the creation of immortal beauty for all time—a combination of gifts which is practically unique in the history of art.

II.—THE ORCHESTRAL WORKS.

In considering Borodin's compositions as a whole one naturally turns first to those for orchestra, for in them we find every characteristic quality which one associates with his name—nationalism, orientalism, lyric beauty, massive structural strength and wealth of colour—each at its best. The Russian creative mind, in seeking inspiration from oriental art (or perhaps through its natural affinity with Eastern mentality) has absorbed two curiously antithetic ideas of beauty—a love of monotony, of endless repetitions and of meditations on the more sombre aspects of nature, and a love of the most vivid, even violent, contrasts of bright colour. Musically, and in the work of Borodin more than in that of any other composer except Stravinsky, these ideas reveal themselves in an escape from the usually accepted ideals, German in origin, of thematic treatment. Put briefly, the Western ideals were to take a theme and, step by step, to develop its possibilities logically and inevitably till its every point was revealed and expounded—orchestral colour being regarded as an additional attraction rather than an essential element in the creative scheme, the manner of expression being always entirely subordinated to the matter expressed. While he rejected these æsthetic standards, however, Borodin never fell into the error, as Rimsky-Korsakov did, of supposing that brilliant orchestration, and a literary or pictorial crutch, in the way of a programme, would cover up deficiencies of thematic and structural strength. In his earlier works, especially, his outlook (thanks to early contact with German medical students, to an affection for Beethoven, Schumann and Mendelssohn (!) and to his travels of 1859-62) was still largely tinged with Western ideas, which obtrude

not a little in the First Symphony, and it was
not until ten years later that he entirely
reached his final standpoint. It may be
noted that to the end of his life he clung
tightly to the classic forms, above all to the
time-honoured "sonata-form," though, unlike Brahms, he is almost always their master and never their mere slave. This
element of classicism was apparently due to
his remarkable and ever-present clarity of
thought and to a dislike for the alien literary elements in symphonic music to which
all other Russian composers have been attracted; his single excursion into the realm
of programme-music, the "Steppenskizze,"
is no such amorphous mass of sound as the
average tone-poem, but a perfectly coherent
symphonic structure.

In the matter of "colour" Borodin was
never actually associated with Rimsky-Korsakov's theories with regard to the affinity
of music and colour, which Scriabin has developed so remarkably in "Prometheus,"
but in the so-called colouring which is pro-

duced by orchestral combinations he has few superiors. Like Rimsky-Korsakov, he preferred brilliant effects, in which one tone-colour stands out vividly from another, to the sonorous, but confused, mixing of tints which is preferred by German orchestrators like Wagner and Strauss, and it is interesting to note that the most modern tendencies follow the Russian, rather than the German, precedent. Borodin's orchestration, at its best, reminds one frequently of a brilliant pattern in mosaic, in which the brightest elementary colours are placed in immediate juxtaposition. The influence of Rimsky-Korsakov is, throughout, so obvious in this respect, that it is not improbable that the latter actually assisted the composer on frequent occasions.. As a matter of fact, he tells us himself, in his autobiography, that he had a hand in the scoring of the Second Symphony, and it is well-known that the orchestral version of Borodin's share of "Mlada" was made by him.

Owing to his numerous scientific and other

extra-musical activities, Borodin left several works in an unfinished state, so that " Prince Igor" was orchestrated by Rimsky-Korsakov and Glazounov, and the fragmentary Third Symphony by Glazounov alone; in discussing these works, then, it is only necessary to consider the scoring of those which were finished by the composer himself. Resting on these alone, his reputation as a master of the orchestra would be exceedingly high, though it must be admitted that the score of even the Second Symphony had to be re-drafted on account of his deficient knowledge of the technique of individual instruments. As has already been mentioned, the First Symphony in E flat was begun in 1862 and was not completed until 1867; though by no means a first composition, it was the first of Borodin's really serious efforts, and even then his technical ability was scarcely equal to the task of symphonic composition. The traces of immaturity were, however, afterwards eradicated by revision. Moussorgsky, rather wrongheadedly, dubbed the symphony "the Russian 'Eroïca,'" in allusion to its place in Borodin's creative career, but Beethoven had progressed considerably farther at his "Eroïca" period than had Borodin when he wrote his E flat Symphony. The work is fairly conventional in form and is scored for a comparatively modest orchestra—two flutes, two oboes, two clarinets, two bassoons, four horns, two trumpets, three trombones, timpani and strings.

The first movement opens with an "adagio" introduction in the tonic minor of twenty-eight bars in length, rather mysterious in feeling and introducing a striking, darkly-coloured theme on bassoons, 'cellos and basses :

Ex. 1.

the last two bars of which are anticipated on the flutes and oboes, and provide the chief material for the introduction, making no further appearance in the rest of the movement.

The "allegro" follows in E flat major, and the composer at once begins to show his ingenuity in the academic methods of theme-development. Ex. 1 is his text (or, rather, the first four bars only of Ex. 1), but instead of re-announcing it in full, in the orthodox way, he dissects it and presents it to us piece by piece. First the timpani take up the figure of the second bar, repeating it again and again, while violins and violas are occupied with bar 3. Then a brassy outburst in which bar 4 is prominent leads to a tutti in which the drum-figure, bar 2, forms the bass. And now for the first time in the "allegro" the theme is heard in a fuller form—bar 4 still being dropped, to reappear later as a bass. The exposition which follows is perfectly orthodox, though very ingenious, but despite the strongly Russian character of the theme, one feels that the mind behind the music is occasionally looking at things from the point of view of a German—a feeling which again strikes one in listening to parts of the First String Quartet, though a much later work; so that, while the music is not at all Tchaï-kovskian in manner or sentiment, the point of view is not dissimilar to that of Tchaïkov-sky's earlier work.

The orchestration is always a perfect joy to listen to, and the climax which precedes the appearance of the second subject is prophetic of the magnificence of the Second Symphony. The second subject, given first to the oboe, is comparatively unimportant.

In the opening of the development the succeeding colours in which Ex. 1 is clothed are very striking. Given first to 'cellos and basses, and then to violas and bassoon, it next flashes out in the bright key of A major on the wood-wind, and finally blazes forth on the brass, with a dazzling string accom-

paniment of tremolo harmonics. After a
time a quieter mood succeeds, introduced by
a brief reference to the second subject. The
drum-figure (bar 2 of Ex. 1) is now given, with
a curiously playful effect to the clarinet, and
afterwards another effective little point is
scored by its reappearance ppp on the drums,
with 'cellos and basses pizzicato. After the
working up of a long-drawn climax the recapitulation follows, but, instead of ending
the movement, this is succeeded by a
long section which is practically a second
development. This gradually piles up
into a tremendous climax, with a quickening of the pace, but, at the end, dies
down into a quiet "andantino" coda in $\frac{3}{2}$
time—an exquisitely poetical conception, in
which one instrument after another meditates
lovingly over Ex. 1 metamorphosed into a
smooth-flowing melody in even note-values.
There are lovely soaring passages for muted
strings (a device of which Borodin was rather
fond) and twice the drums throb out their old
figure rather drowsily without in the least

disturbing the tranquillity of the whole. The
prestissimo Scherzo, superficially attractive
as it is, is on the whole weak; good enough
light music, perhaps, but it belongs too much
to the Beethovenian order of things to be
quite congruent in a symphony by Borodin.
It is chiefly concerned with flying figures in
$\frac{3}{8}$ time on violins and violas, which are caught
up by the wood-wind, with a piquant pizzi-
cato accompaniment.   Other themes, rather
slight in value, are introduced, and the whole
is carried out with great wit and skill in orchestration, but it is only in the trio, an "allegro" in B major, that the real Borodin appears.   Over a tonic pedal the oboes and a
clarinet play a folk-song-like melody:

Ex. 2.

etc.

which, in its treatment, is interesting as foreshadowing the composer's later methods,
i.e., of reiteration of themes in varying forms
rather than in development as the word is
usually understood. The alternation of
triple and common time is prominent almost
throughout, and the richness of scoring and
of the harmonies is very prophetic. One of
the most striking effects is produced by a
pizzicato accompaniment figure which Moussorgsky described as " pecking," and another
delightful passage, just preceding the return
of the *prestissimo*, is that in which Ex. 2 is
treated " conversationally" between the
wood-wind instruments over a syncopated,
throbbing pedal-note on the string basses.

The slow movement, an " andante " in
D major (the tonality of the whole symphony
is very free) is also prophetic in its strongly
Oriental flavouring, to enhance which a cor
anglais is substituted for the second oboe
(the trumpets and trombones being silent
throughout). The whole of the first section

is composed of a long-drawn melody for
the 'cellos :

Ex. 3.

p cantabile ed espress

etc.

which afterwards flowers out in arabesque or-
naments and is continued on flute and cor
anglais.   After a short cadenza for the latter
instrument, the 'cellos play another melody
of a quasi-Oriental nature, which is taken up
by the violins.   There is a brief reference to
Ex. 3 on the cor anglais, and then the drums
settle down on a quiet, monotonous figure,
which pervades the rest of this section and
decidedly heightens the Eastern flavour of
the music.   After this a return is made to
Ex. 3, now played *forte* by the wood-wind
in octaves, and the movement ends quietly
with a long-drawn syncopated pedal D on
violas, 'cellos and horns.

The Finale, a decidedly undistinguished
"allegro molto vivo," is a thoroughly occi-
dental piece of orthodoxy. Dr. Oscar
Riesemann thinks it Schumannesque, and it
certainly has a considerable affinity with
some of that composer's symphonic movements—the first of the B flat Symphony and
the Finale of the "Rhenish," for instance.

It opens with a vigorous theme:

Ex. 4.

given to the strings in unison and is carried
through to the end in that mood of boister-
ous high-spirits which so often disguises the
weaknesses of second rate music. The
second subject is not sufficiently striking to
save the situation and even the orchestration,
another of the average composer's ever present helps in time of trouble, is very commonplace—for Borodin. The sonata form
is strictly adhered to—even to the extent of

M. P. MOUSSORGSKY.

(By permission of M P. Belaieff, St. Petersburg.)

repeating the exposition—and the working-out of the themes is thoroughly traditional in method. The only point of real interest occurs near the end where Ex. 4 is treated as a bass—thundered out on trombones, etc., in a broad *fff* "maestoso" tutti of genuine, if slightly vulgar, strength and power, yet strangely inferior to the tuttis of Borodin's later work.

Viewed as a whole the symphony is lacking in cohesive unity, its architecture resembling that of a nouveau riche drawing-room in its patchwork of various styles. The reason lies, of course, in Borodin's immaturity, *as a creative artist*, not in technical immaturity of which there is little or no trace in the whole of the work. It must be admitted, nevertheless, that the symphony probably owed a great deal of its immediate popularity in Germany to the fact that its idiom was still, in part, that of the common herd of western Romantics of the period, and won an acceptance for itself and a name for its composer, which might have been denied to a work by an unknown composer wholly expressed in terms of a totally different musicality.

Such a work, however, is the Second Symphony, than which no more thoroughly Russian music has ever been written. Owing its inspiration to the trains of thought engendered by the researches into a remote period of Russian history undertaken in the preparation of "Mlada" and "Prince Igor," one can, as Stassov said, hear in it a re-echoing of the spirit of Russia's heroic age, noble and barbarous. Felix Weingartner, who considers it the most important production of modern Russian music, says, in "Die Symphonie nach Beethoven," that it conveys a perfect picture of Russian life and character. Yet any impression that its strength is at all dependent on any pictorial, or other, crutch, would be quite erroneous; as a well known English critic wrote of it, a year or two ago: "If there is a more perfect example of felicitous construction in music, on traditional lines, allied with a consummate

sense of orchestral colour combinations and
a power of thematic invention which is
nothing short of what the Germans call
'genial,' in the whole range of modern
music, I have yet to make its acquaintance."
It is, indeed, a work of which it is difficult to
speak without appearing to hyperbolise. Its
very key is not without interest—B minor,
which Beethoven considered a *"black* key"
and generally avoided. That there is a good
deal of rich, purple "blackness" in Borodin's
first movement (the only one in the chief key
of the symphony) is certainly true, while the
"blackness" in a different sense, of another
Russian symphony in that key—Tchaïkovsky's Sixth, the notorious "Pathétique"—is
a byword among the nations.

For this work, too, the composer has en-
larged his orchestral palette, the forces required for its performance including three
flutes (one alternating with piccolo), two
oboes (one of which changes to cor anglais
in the slow movement), two clarinets, two
bassoons, four horns, two trumpets, three

trombones, tuba, three timpani, triangle,
tambourine, bass drum and cymbals (in the
finale only), harp and strings.

The symphony begins without any introduction, with an immediate statement of the
main theme on all the strings in octaves :

Ex. 5.

a magnificently barbaric gesture which has
only to be heard to impress itself indelibly
upon the imagination. The pace is
"allegro," but almost immediately, with a
sudden fierce quickening of the *tempo*,
comes an important pendant on the wood-
wind, full of savage, primitive joy :

Ex. 6.

etc.

the element of sheer, stark reiteration which is such a characteristic feature of the symphony being as prominent in this theme as in Ex. 5. There are powerful syncopations on the brass, alternating with sforzando chords for strings and wood-wind, and again Ex. 5 returns in all its crude force, now passionately, desperately striving, now confidently driving home its heroic hammer blows with mighty, giant strength. It is impossible to hear this music and not be conscious that one is listening to an expression of precisely the same elemental feelings which have found a more modern utterance in the "rhythmic tramplings" of "Le Sacre du Printemps." The second subject, "poco meno mosso," is lyrical in character, but, though of great beauty, it never assumes sufficient importance to afford more than a transitory relief. It is given first to the 'cellos, then to the wood-wind and, after a brief appearance on the upper strings, is then swept into the faster *tempo* of the prevailing mood of the movement.

In the development, again, Ex. 5 reigns all-powerful. Its treatment is new and striking in orchestration, as, for instance, when at the beginning it is given in turn to clarinet, bassoon and oboe soli, taking on quite a new character, but there is scarcely any of what is usually understood by the word "development," namely, the logical exploitation of themes. That Borodin was not merely able to treat his themes in the orthodox way, but particularly skilful in such treatment we know from the evidence of the first movement of the First Symphony (to say nothing of some of his other works; but, in this case, his mind seems to return again and again to the same point, viewing it from different angles, instead of moving definitely forward from one position to another in the western way. Borodin's semi-oriental mentality is never more fully revealed than in this movement, and, as Grove said, "the first movement always more or less gives its *cachet* to a symphony."

After a time a new rhythmic figure

is introduced by the drums and soon pervades the whole fabric, Ex. 5 being worked
against it. After references to Ex. 6 and to
the second subject, this figure, now on F
sharp, is treated as a pedal on a kettledrum,
above which the trombones and trumpets in-
tone Ex. 5 with particularly sombre effect.

In the recapitulation, reached by a brilliant, climactic passage, the note-values of Ex.
5 (blazed out *fff* by the full orchestra) are
doubled. This section is considerably con-
densed but at the end, comes a magnificently
coloured coda, in which the rhythmic figure,
previously alluded to, recurs, and which concludes with a very broad final enunciation of
Ex. 5, *fff* on strings, wood-wind and brass in
unison, terrifying in its emphasis.

The exceedingly brilliant and individual
scherzo is in the distant key of F major,
reached by a modulatory passage, devised
by Balakirev, which did not appear in Boro-

din's original score. The most striking
feature of this glittering movement is the
rapid and incessant reiteration of a single
note, at first a C on the horns, which persists
almost throughout, the *tempo* being "prestissimo" and the time signature ¼ (four
crotchets in a bar). There are scintillating
outbursts on wood-wind and pizzicato
strings, which resemble clouds of flying
spray, or rather, perhaps, the showers of
sparks from a brilliant firework; another
somewhat pyrotechnic effect is that of a constantly recurring syncopated passage in
which only the string basses and bass trombone are on the beat, while the full weight
of strings, wind and bass is thrown on the
unaccented part of each bar. Any quotation
of the rather slight thematic material of the
movement would be of little use, for it de-
pends almost entirely for its effect upon the
glitter and sparkle of its remarkably brilliant
scoring, at the time it was written unpar-
alleled in symphonic literature and even now

undimmed by comparison with the works of
even the finest modern orchestrators.

Gradually the music becomes quieter and
its last flying fragments die away into the
"allegretto" trio, which is in striking contrast to that which has preceded it. A solo
oboe sings out a limpid melody, "cantabile
e dolce":

Ex. 7.

to which the *ppp* accompaniment of harp
and triangle gives a delightful spring-like
freshness. This is continued very beautifully on the other wood-wind instruments
and horns, and later by the strings. After a
final broadly flowing version of Ex. 7 on
flutes, first violins and 'cellos, accompanied
by pizzicato and harp chords, a return is
made to the silvery, flashing "prestissimo."

This scherzo, one of the most striking and individual movements Borodin ever wrote, is in perfect harmony with the prevailing heroic mood of the whole symphony, suggesting, if one may be permitted the simile, the gleam of sunlight upon the helmets of Slavonic warriors. The slow movement, an "andante" in D flat, is introduced by a lovely phrase on a solo clarinet accompanied by harp chords. The chief melody, one of melting beauty, announced by a solo horn:

Ex. 8.

is accompanied by strings and harp, and is afterwards transferred to the clarinet—its first motif "A" recurring again and again throughout the movement, as a sort of motto theme. A slightly quicker section is built up from a *motif*, rather Oriental in character:

Ex. 9.

on the solo wood wind instruments and horns, and accompanied by a divided string tremolo, and then, after a rather unexpected broad enunciation of Ex. 8a on the full orchestra, fortissimo, the third subject makes its appearance on the strings :

Ex. 10.

the chromatic counter subject always being associated with it. A short development of Exs. 8 and 10 leads to a big climax for the full orchestra and then after references to Ex. 9 on cor anglais and clarinets, the three themes are repeated in the same order as that in which they appeared first but quite differently treated—Ex. 8 now being given

to flute, oboe, cor anglais and strings in unison, while Ex. 9 is accompanied by an Oriental arabesque melody on the first violins.
Ex. 10 completes the mood of contemplation and contentment which is the key-note
of this last section and the movement ends,
on a point of perfect repose, with the clarinet
phrase with which it opened while the horn
replies dreamily with the *motif* A from Ex.
8, the absolute tranquillity of the whole
being deepened by a *pianissimo* drum roll.
This movement, while without the least trace
of extra musical significance is as remarkable as anything of Tchaïkovsky's or Scriabin's in its revelation of the composer's mind
and soul; it is a draught of pure beauty,
apparently inspired by nothing more (or
rather, nothing less) than that longing to
create something of corresponding, inexpressible loveliness which is produced by
contemplation of the natural beauties of
one's native land. Like Vaughan Williams
at times, Borodin seems here to be trying to
distil the essence of all that is truest and

noblest in patriotism, and, like the Englishman he has wonderfully expressed this most
soul-stirring of passions in music of pro-
found tranquillity.   The Finale in B major,
from beginning to end a gorgeous pageant
of barbaric colour, is ingeniously connected
with the preceding movement by an A flat—D
flat on the second violins which now becomes
enharmonically G sharp—C sharp.   There at
once appears an eager, syncopated figure on
the lower strings in which the wind immediately join and which recurs at various points
in the movement.   The chief *motif*, heroic in
character, is announced by the upper
strings :

Ex. 11.

and almost immediately there follows the
first of those floods of rich orchestral colour
which are the most memorable feature of the
movement—here only a foretaste of what is
to come and the prelude to a much greater
one, an outburst of fiery magnificence in

which Ex. 11 blazes out in regal pomp and
splendour. It fades out gradually, though
still bathed in rich orchestral and harmonic
colours which seem like the warm reflection
of what has just been heard, only to flame
out again with all the force of wood-wind,
brass and percussion. The key now
changes, first to D major, and after a few
bars a solo clarinet introduces the second
subject:

Ex. 12.

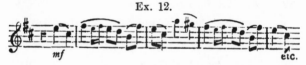

It is repeated in the sharp, brilliant tones of
piccolo and oboe, and then it too, in a
slightly varied form, assumes gorgeous trap-
pings and is crashed out like a great pagan
hymn to Nature. Gradually the mood softens
and the development is introduced by final
references to Ex. 12 on the various wood-
wind instruments solo.

The trombones now bring us back to the
mood of the first movement, by their "mar-

cato e pesante" announcements of a theme
which is really derived from Ex. 11, but now
"lento" in time. After this, in turn, has
been worked up to the inevitable climax, Ex.
12 assumes prominence; first, with the feeling of some pagan rite, on all the strings in
octaves, "pesante," and then in the form we
have heard once before with all the overwhelming power of the full orchestra.

Of the recapitulation it is needless to
speak; musically, it is quite orthodox and
after all, no analysis or description can convey more than a faint impression of the barbaric splendour of this great canvas of
sound. It must be, inevitably, interpreted
(if interpretation be required) as an apotheosis of Russia's ancient glory, while, as
music, it is simply monumental; the dazzling
incandescence of the actual conclusion can
only be equalled by that of Scriabin's
" Prometheus."

In spite of the contrasting natures of each
individual movement and its parts, the symphony impresses one, above all, by the

absolute unity of its conception. Although
its composition was spread over a period of
several years and interrupted by other and
very different work, it conveys the impression of having been conceived immediately
as a finite whole; an impression which is
heightened by the rich and brilliantly original orchestration and by the similarity to
type of so many of its melodies, all of which,
while not actual folk-tunes, perfectly reproduce the essential feeling as well as the more
superficial features of Russian folk-music.
Formally, the work, as is almost always the
case with Borodin, is cast in those classic
moulds which, in the hands of true genius,
are still at once the most elastic and the most
satisfying known to musicians; for sonata-
form, whatever the hot-headed musical re-
volutionaries may say, is no mere fetter to
the imagination, but rather a plastic and
balanced framework upon which the composer is at liberty to build almost as he
wishes. Any musical movement which is not
based upon the principles of balance and

contrast which, in their most imposing development, are what we call sonata-form, is amorphous; that is, it is lacking in those faculties of selection and orderliness which are all that differentiate genius from insanity. Yet Borodin, despite this perfect and never-failing coherence of his, did not escape the usual academic parrot-cry of "iconoclasm"; and one is left with a bewildering uncertainty as to which is the more insane—the Right or the Left in musical politics.

At the time of his death Borodin was working at a Third Symphony—in A minor. Two movements were practically finished, and these were completed and orchestrated by Alexander Glazounov with considerable sympathy for the composer's methods and intentions. While it cannot be said that these fragments show an advance on the Second Symphony, they are, in a different way, equally characteristic. The folk-song influence is as prominent as ever, and the

clarity and strength of form and harmony
are, if anything, greater than ever.

The first movement, an almost placid
"moderato assai," is as entirely genial and
untroubled as the corresponding movement
of its predecessor is forceful and energetic;
in mood, but in nothing else, one is reminded
forcibly of the opening of Tchaïkovsky's
little-known First Symphony ("Winter Day-
Dreams"), and the sub-title of its first movement—"Dreams on the High-road." The
opening melody announced unaccompanied:

Ex. 13.

p a piacere

poco rit.

is of the nature of what a modern British
composer would call a "walking-tune," and
its later treatment with incessant repetitions,
either of the whole tune or of shorter snatches

of it, inevitably suggests the tranquil contentment of a country-walk, which, in conjunction with the even, mechanical rhythm
of the feet, will inspire the most unmusical
to some effort at melody.   Ex. 13 is immediately followed, on its first appearance, by a
pendant :

Ex. 14.

etc.

which is of considerable importance, but for
the present the music is chiefly concerned
with Ex. 13, treated in ways which suggest a
charming instrumental " conversation." A
moderate climax is soon worked up and leads
to some full repetitions of Ex. 14, which is
then used as the material for a sonorous
bridge-passage of breadth and dignity,
modulating to E major, the key of the
second subject. The latter, in slightly
slower *tempo*, richly harmonised :

Ex. 15.

etc.

introduces a new note of warm colour into
the music as if reverie had taken another
turn, though in what direction each listener
must judge for himself; there is a hint of
national pride and regal dignity—neither
ever far in the background of Borodin's
larger canvases.

After a time the pace is quickened, and
the latter part of Ex. 15—bar 5 *et seq.*—
becomes prominent in the bass, thus leading
up to the very short development section.
The latter, despite its undeniable beauty, is
rather weak, and would probably have not
been allowed to remain in this state had the
composer lived.   As it is, it consists almost

entirely of alternations and combinations of
Exs. 13 and 15 over a pedal-note—first an
F sharp and then an E—and has the effect of
being a mere interlude before the recapitulation begins. This follows the usual course,
both the bridge-passage on Ex. 14 and the
second subject, Ex. 15, being in A major, in
which key the movement ends. Mention,
however, must be made of the very beautiful
coda, "sostenuto e tranquillo," which brings
the music to a point of perfect repose. The
final dying-away of bar one of Ex. 13 is exquisitely coloured, and the poetry of the
whole is considerably heightened by Glazounov's delicately tinted scoring, like soft,
refined water-colours, to which the harmonics
of the strings give the purest ethereality.

The Scherzo, in D major, was, apparently,
like its predecessors of the First and Second
Symphonies, to form the second movement
of the work instead of succeeding the slow
movement, and is particularly interesting as
being almost the only instance of Borodin's
use of quintuple time. Really original

scherzi are not easy to write, but this one is
as entirely off the beaten track as that of the
B minor Symphony, without being in the
least like it.   Its opening, an accompaniment
figure on the notes D, A, E, the open strings
of the violin, recalls the introduction to
Moussorgsky's well-known "Gopak," from
"The Fair of Sorotchinsky," with its realistic "tuning-up," but the movement as a
whole is entirely dominated by a bustling
"vivo" figure :

Ex. 16.

treated in various ways with the greatest ingenuity.   Sometimes it is worked as a bass
and sometimes with fresh counter-subjects—
the whole forming an exceedingly brilliant
orchestral moto perpetuo.

The Trio, a "moderato," in $\frac{3}{4}$ time, is in
complete contrast. A melody of a decidedly
folk-songish character :

Ex. 17.

provides the material for a very beautiful
interlude of almost naïve simplicity of feeling—one of those lovely pages which Russian composers sometimes give us, in which
one is content to enjoy melody for its own
sake and forget the mastery of technique
which alone can permit of such ingenuous-
ness.   As the last echoes of Ex. 17 die away
in the bass the sparkling moto perpetuo returns and continues its vivid, flashing course
to the brilliant final climax.   Judging from
these two movements, polished by another,
if sympathetic, hand, one can have no hesitation in affirming that the Third Symphony, if
completed, would have been a really great
work; not such an outstanding, challenging
masterpiece as his Second, certainly, but still
a work as worthy of Borodin as the Fourth

and Eighth Symphonies are of Beethoven. It would probably have been as wholly light-hearted and idyllic in character as the B minor is epic, and there is as much room in our art for the one thing as for the other.

Of Borodin's orchestral works the next in importance to the symphonies is that extremely popular concert-piece, the so-called "symphonic sketch," "On the Steppes of Central Asia," which, as the only instance of the composer's harnessing his imagination to a definite programme (and a not particularly original one, at that) is extremely interesting; the dedication to Liszt is rather appropriate for the latter was, at that time, the chief living exponent of the tone-poem. The original function of the piece was as a sort of musical accompaniment to one of a series of historical *tableaux vivants* which formed part of the celebrations of the silver jubilee of the Czar Alexander II, in 1880, but it is certainly on a far higher artistic level than the average *pièce d'occasion*.

The programmatic basis of the work may

be given as follows: "The silence of the sandy steppes of Central Asia is interrupted by the first sounds of a peaceful Russian song. Then the melancholy refrain of an Oriental song is heard, and with it the tramp of horses and camels. A caravan escorted by Russian soldiers is crossing the immense desert, fearlessly continuing its long journey under the protection of the Russian troops. The caravan proceeds on its way. The songs of the Russians and those of the Asiatics gradually blend together in the same harmony; their refrains are heard for some time and finally die away in the distance."

The "approaching-and-passing" idea is, of course, rather hackneyed, but it has the advantage of being balanced and straightforward,* and, considered as purely abstract music, the piece is so soundly constructed that no knowledge of the programme is really necessary to enjoy it.

The music opens *pp* with a high E in oc-

---

* The prelude to "Lohengrin" is a similar example of perfectly balanced programme-music.

taves, for two solo violins, gradually joined
by the rest in pairs, which is sustained for
over fifty bars as an inverted pedal.   The
first theme, the Russian one, appears first on
a solo clarinet :

Ex. 18.

and then on a solo horn.   Next there is introduced a striking pizzicato bass-figure on
'cellos and basses which persists in one
form or another throughout the piece, and is
obviously intended to suggest the dull tramp-
ling of horses and camels.   The second
(Oriental) subject :

Ex. 19.

is not long in making its appearance. With its monotonous pedal-bass it is somewhat closely related to the melody of the opening number of Act II of " Prince Igor,"* and is given to the cor anglais—the only "extra" instrument introduced in the comparatively modest score. The cor anglais solo is continued at some length, and then the music is again chiefly concerned with Ex. 18, first on the wood-wind, next on the horns (accompanied by full, rich trombone chords), and finally thundered out *ff* on the full orchestra —the only tutti in the whole work.

After a gradual *decrescendo*, Ex. 19 returns with all its monotonous, brooding sadness on 'celli and cor anglais in unison. Up to this point the music, while interesting and attractive, has not reached great heights, but now a sudden magical modulation from A minor to A major, seems to transfigure it with warm beauty, like a quick ray of sunlight darting through coloured glass. Ex. 19,

---

* See Ex. 23.

now on the violins, is invested with a new
richness, its melancholy tinged with a sweetness which is almost sentimental, and
scarcely diminished by the deeper and fuller
sonority of violas and 'cellos.   And now
Ex. 18 returns again, on the plaintive oboe,
while Ex. 19 continues in counterpoint below
it—a combination which continues with rich
and varied scoring for some time; then the
positions are reversed—Ex. 19 being given
to flutes and violins, and Ex. 18 to violas,
'cellos and cor anglais.

From this point the music gradually dies
away, as the caravan seems to disappear in
the distance—the repeated echoes of Ex. 18
being charmingly coloured by harmony and
orchestration in a way that probably suggested the similar effect that closes the first
movement of the A minor Symphony.

Finally the fragments of the melody, its
repetitions overlapping as if confused by
distance, become quite extinct; four muted
violins again sound the ethereal high E
which opens the movement, and then a solo

flute plays Ex. 18 once more in full, pp
"dolcissimo"—like a reminiscent echo in the
mind of the listener.

There is no doubt that the "Steppenskizze" is a very attractive little work and
one well-calculated to catch the ear of the
man-in-the-street; the latter gentleman
always likes something with a tune in it, and,
if possible, something with a story in it, and
he gets *both* in this case. The workmanship
is clever enough to interest the musician and
the thematic material is quite typical of the
composer, so that one's only objection to its
popularity is that the average concert-goer is
in danger of being led to forget the existence
of Borodin's greater works. It may be mentioned in passing that Borodin probably took
the hint for his method of thematic treatment
(first presenting the subjects separately and
then combining them) from Glinka's "Kamarinskaia," in which a similar procedure is
adopted; Borodin, however, was always fond
of theme-combination and employs the de-

vice in quite a number of his works—the
First String Quartet being a particularly fine
example.

One of Borodin's latest compositions was
an orchestral Scherzo in A flat, dedicated to
his admirer, Jadoul, a friend of the previ-
ously-mentioned Countess Mercy-Argenteau;
it is not particularly characteristic of the
composer, being more in the manner of his
friend Cui, and, though made attractive by
its wit and light-handed scoring, is rather
slight in value.

Its chief theme is a flying "allegro vivace"
figure :

Ex. 20.

etc.

but a little four-note chromatic *motif*, which
may be considered as a sort of second subject, assumes considerable importance, its
treatment being very ingenious.   Instead of
a Trio there is a brief development section

in which Ex. 20 is worked up to an energetic *fortissimo* climax. The recapitulation follows in due course, the end of the piece being particularly piquant, but one is never conscious of the presence of the real Borodin. Its place in his output is quite unimportant.

III.—WORKS FOR THE STAGE.

As we have already seen, Borodin's first venture in the sphere of dramatic music, "La Fiancée du Tsar," was a failure and abandoned by the composer, as such, before he had made much progress with the music, so that his first really serious composition for the stage was the last act of the opera-ballet, "Mlada"—a work which had its origin in rather peculiar circumstances.

The operatic theories of the "Invincible Band" being well-known, it occurred to Etienne Guédéonov, the director of the Imperial Russian Opera, that a joint-work by its members would be interesting—and, incidentally, provocative of that curiosity which is an infallible guarantee of financial

CÉSAR CUI.

(By permission of M. P. Belaieff, St. Petersburg.)

success. To that end he prepared a really excellent libretto on the subject of a ninth-century Baltic legend, with enormous scope for spectacular effects and national atmosphere and colour, a "book" which accorded in every way with the ideals and tenets of the "Kouchka," and which was, accordingly, very willingly accepted by them towards the end of 1871. The work was in four acts, the first being allotted to Cui, the second to Rimsky-Korsakov, the third to Moussorgsky, and the fourth to Borodin, while the ballet-music was to be provided by a fifth collaborator of very different calibre, Minkus, who seems curiously out of place in such company; a division of labour only surpassed by that required to produce a modern revue, which boded ill for the homogeneity of the resultant work. But, in spite of the number of cooks employed in its preparation, the broth came to nothing. The cost of production was seen to be out of all proportion to the probable chances of recoupment, and the enterprising Guédéonov was compelled

to resign his directorship.   His libretto was
not, however, wasted; for, some twenty years
later, Rimsky-Korsakov again returned to it
and utilised the whole for one of his finest
operas.

Of the music written in 1871, Moussorgsky's contribution is best known for its
partial identity with his earlier orchestral
fantasia, "Une Nuit sur le Mont-Chauve,"
one of his most popular concert-pieces. Borodin's portion of the work was, however,
acknowledged to be decidedly the best, and
Rimsky-Korsakov, with that admirable freedom from jealousy so characteristic of every
member of the group, rescued it from ob-
livion   after   the   composer's   death   by
producing part of it in a concert version for
orchestra alone, as a sort of "symphonic picture," in which form we must accept it for
want of a better.

The plot of "Mlada" is a rather complicated affair in which the element of the
supernatural plays a very important part.
The hero, Prince Jaromir, is in love with the

wicked Voïslava, a princess of Rhétra, who, unknown to him, has poisoned his former betrothed, Mlada, on the eve of their wedding. Although informed in a dream of Voïslava's guilt, he is unable to quench his passion for her, till, at last, the spirit of Mlada herself appears and bears him away to the other world. Jaromir now understands everything, and, returning to earth, kills the false Voïslava, who is carried away, body and soul, by the infernal goddess Morena, at whose instigation she has committed her crimes. The goddess now seeks to avenge her death, and proceeds to bring about a great convulsion of all the destructive powers of nature, in the hope of destroying her human enemies. The winds and waters rise in a tremendous tempest in which even the temple of Radegast, god of light, is submerged, but, in the end, the powers of darkness are vanquished and the spirit of Mlada appears in the sky—after the manner of Senta and the Flying Dutchman.

It is with this last part of the story that

the surviving portion of Borodin's music
deals, and from it we must be content to de-
duce the rest.   The opening "allegro
furioso" is introduced by a portentous drum-
roll, and deals very realistically with the con-
jurations of the enraged goddess, in a
manner similar to that of Liadov's "Baba-
Yaga" or some of Moussorgsky's essays in
the supernatural.   The music has a certain
weird effectiveness which would probably be
successful enough in the sphere for which it
was intended—the theatre, but, as concert-
music, it is decidedly unconvincing.   So, too,
with the "storm"; its vivid realism and the
skill with which it is gradually worked up to
a tremendous cataclysm at its climactic point
are undeniable, but the music is too much of
the theatre, too insincere to be really worthy
of Borodin.   Its merely superficial power
and brilliance are the more remarkable when
we remember that it was written contempor-
aneously with the great Symphony in B
minor; it is not even particularly individual,
for the influence of Moussorgsky is strongly

apparent, while some passages are obviously
closely copied from the stormier pages of
Balakirev's "Thamar." One interesting
point, however, is the frequent recurrence in
this section of a sinister theme :

Ex. 21.

treated as a sort of leitmotiv, which has been
heard first in the invocation scene, and seems
to be intended to express Morena's curse
upon Jaromir. After a time the storm gradually dies down, after the manner of most
musical storms, the *tempo* changes to "andantino," and the apotheosis of Mlada
commences in the manner of most musical
apotheoses—with arpeggios on the harp. An
expressive, flowing melody in A flat now appears, "dolce," and provides the material for
the conclusion, which is impressed with real
beauty though by no means on a level with
Borodin's finest work. Of course, it must be
remembered before condemning the music of
"Mlada" entirely that we have no means,

except imagination, of judging it in its
proper surroundings with all the advantages
of scenic effect—though stage pictures are no
excuse for, if a palliation of, poor music.
Further it must not be forgotten that the
music, as we know it, passed through the
hands of Rimsky-Korsakov, who, as we
know from his versions of "Boris
Godounov" and Khovantchina," was possessed with a mania for "touching-up" (in
none too good taste, if with the best intentions) as incorrigible as that of our own Victorian Prince Consort. "Prince Igor,"
Borodin's only complete opera, also passed
through Rimsky-Korsakov's editorially im-
proving hand, this time assisted by that of
his pupil, Glazounov, before it saw the light
of public performance in 1890—three years
after its creator's death. In this case, however, much of the music is of a very different
order.

As has already been stated Borodin first
turned his attention to the subject of this
work as early as 1871, at the suggestion of

Stassov, but worked at it so intermittently that it was still uncompleted at his death. From the historical point of view and from that of truth of local colour and atmosphere the work is almost perfect, but, unfortunately, in order to ensure such entire accuracy and such sympathy with the subject as he felt imperative Borodin was compelled to follow the Wagnerian precedent and become his own librettist. One says "unfortunately" advisedly, for it is entirely to the weaknesses of the "book" that the comparative failure of the work to hold the stage in western Europe is due. The whole action, spread over a prologue and four acts, is, as Mr. Montagu-Nathan says, "singularly lacking in dramatic interest." The plot is practically non-existent and treated in such a thoroughly unsatisfactory way that a fifth act seems to be needed to bring the work to a definite conclusion. The villain of the piece disappears altogether after the first act and indeed the whole drama consists of a succession of isolated scenes connected by the

weakest of threads—an objection which may
also be levelled against Moussorgsky's
"Boris Godounov." To crown all, the plot
has for the ordinary western opera-going
public the appalling disadvantage of being
conspicuously deficient in events of a mur-
derous, or otherwise violent, nature. The
handicap of such a dramatically unsatisfactory libretto could not fail to affect the musical treatment of it and one feels the latter to
be, stylistically, in the nature of a compromise. Naturally drawn, as he himself
tells us, to genuine singing melody rather
than to declamatory recitative Borodin's
sympathies were, from the first, with Glinka
rather than Dargomijsky, and his music
falls, therefore, very largely into the old-
fashioned divisions, the unreal "set numbers" of Italian opera, sometimes connected
without any break, it is true, but even then in
a merely arbitrary fashion and without any
genuinely musical cohesion. At times a
more modern and individual elaboration of
treatment is employed, not without success,

and the occasional use of a phrase as a leit
motif reminds one that the music is supposed
to have some organic connection but, viewed
as a whole and from the purely musical point
of view, "Prince Igor" is curiously
amorphous.

It must be clearly understood too, that
owing to the lyrical nature of the treatment,
the orchestra is in the great bulk of the work,
quite subordinated to the voices—a proceed-
ing which seems nearer to dramatic truth
than Wagner's method of turning the *orchestra* into the chief actor or rather into all the
actors by turns. In this respect "Prince
Igor" conformed entirely to the lines laid
down by the "Band" in their original plans
for a new, national opera; so too, it did in the
employment of elaborate stage pageantry
and in the thoroughly national character of
much of the music, so that there is little
wonder that, despite the conventionality of
the actual structure, the work was received
with unmixed praise by the other members of
the little group. Their rules were not of cast

iron and they had the sense to recognise that each must find his own means of artistic salvation, so to speak. Borodin, as we have already seen in studying his symphonic compositions, had more of the evolutionary improver of accepted conventions than of the daring, iconoclastic innovator in his mental composition, so that it is unreasonable to demand of him the experimental strokes of genius of a Moussorgsky. Above all his nature was really entirely antagonistic to anything approaching the dramatic, so that we must be content to regard " Prince Igor " merely as a fine series of related stage pictures rather than as a genuinely dramatic work, but viewed as such, there is no contesting its beauty and magnificence.

The work is preceded by a fairly lengthy overture in regular form, deriving the whole of its thematic material from various numbers in the opera, and which may therefore be best described last of all. The prologue is introduced by a short "andante maestoso" passage in the orchestra which reaches a climax

at the rise of the curtain. The scene is laid
in a public square of the town of Poutivle,
thronged with Russian troops whose immin-
ent departure for war is being acclaimed by
the townspeople. It is the year 1185, and the
land has been harried by the Polovtsi, noma-
dic hordes of barbarians from the east; these
have already been defeated by Svïatoslav,
Prince of Kiev, and now the latter's son,
Igor, Prince of Seversk (baritone), is preparing to complete the overthrow. As the curtain rises, Igor, accompanied by his subor-
dinate princes and boyards, comes out in
state from the cathedral in which he has been
praying for the success of his arms and is
greeted by the townspeople in a stirring
"allegro moderato e maestoso" chorus :

Ex. 22.

full of breadth and colour. The crowd sings
the praises of the Russian hero princes and
of the brave warriors who fight under their

banners and Igor, in turn, encourages his soldiers to the battle.

Suddenly the brilliant scene is interrupted by a *pp* drum roll; an eclipse of the sun is beginning and the stage gradually darkens. The weird effect is accentuated in the orchestra by sullen drum-rolls and sinister progressions of heavy, shifting chords and the chorus, naturally taking the phenomenon as an evil omen for Igor's project, begs him to give up the undertaking. The Prince, however, refuses to be discouraged and calls upon them to disregard the portent and follow him, but still some of his nobles hang back and counsel prudence and it is not until the daylight has fully returned (a very "unastronomically" rapid eclipse!) that confidence is generally restored.

Prince Igor having retired to the back of the stage with his nobles, to review his troops, the humorous element is introduced by a little exhibition of cowardice on the part of Eroschka (tenor) and Skoula (bass), two players on the "goudok" (a national instrument, obviously introduced to heighten the "local colour"), who finally throw away their arms and sneak quietly off in the hope of getting safer employment than fighting. A succession of quiet chords is now heard as Igor calls for the ladies to come and take their farewells; his wife, Jaroslavna (soprano) rushes to him and passionately begs him to stay with her in safety, but he stresses the call of duty and strives to allay her superstitious forebodings. Vladimir (tenor), his son by a former marriage, is impatient to be off and Igor finally confides his wife to the care of her brother, Prince Vladimir Galitsky (bass), whom he has previously befriended and who is now to act as regent in his absence. Jaroslavna, with the other noble ladies, makes her exit accompanied by the same succession of solemn chords which heralded her approach and Igor approaches an old seer, who at his request, blesses the troops. The prince and his nobles then place themselves at the head of the army and

the curtain falls after a repetition of the
massive opening chorus, Ex. 22.

The first act, which is entirely concerned with the happenings in Poutivle
after Igor's departure, is divided into
two scenes. The first takes place in the
courtyard of the house of Prince Vladimir
Galitsky, who has seized the oppor-
tunity afforded by his newly-obtained power
to gratify his lust and cruelty. As the curtain rises a festive phrase, much repeated, is
heard in the orchestra and the menfolk who
are filling the courtyard burst into a boister-
ous chorus in praise of Galitsky, whose free,
licentious rule is obviously preferred by them
to that of Igor; Eroschka and Skoula, now
in the pay of the regent, mingle with them in
the rôle of mischief-makers.

Galitsky himself appears and after a typically lyrical recitative in which he makes
liberal promises of laxity of government
when he has completely usurped his absent
brother-in-law's power, breaks into an aria of
the conventional operatic type, though musi-

cally on a far higher level than the usual one
of such effusions, in the same vein. This
contradiction of musical manner and matter
is prevalent almost throughout the work; in
a composition of this nature the definite symmetrical form of such a number is as unreal
and out-of-date as the extraordinarily unani-
mous outbursts of the chorus, yet like the
latter it is almost redeemed by the quite
novel and attractive flavour of the music
itself.

The crowd applaud the usurper and he is
about to make his exit when he is arrested by
the entrance of a number of girls who complain that his men have carried off one of
their number. Galitsky not only refuses to
listen to their complaints but tells them that
the abduction has actually been carried out
by his orders and drives them from his presence—all to a suave, somewhat folk-songish
melody which is as attractive as any in the
work; Borodin seems not to have made the
least attempt at musical characterisation of
personalities at any point, though there is a

very strong differentiation between the music
allotted to the Russians and that associated
with the eastern Polovtsi. Galitsky's ser-
vants now roll in a cask of wine and, led by
the two goudok players, proceed to make
merry, after which they sing another chorus
in honour of the prince, whom they now
openly wish to place on the throne of the
absent Igor. The whole of the music of this
latter scene carries out the feeling of boister-
ous gaiety without falling into the mere vulgar banality which such scenes usually call
forth, and the whole is rounded off by the re-
introduction towards the end, of the festive
measure on which the curtain rose. Once
again the two buffoons provide the "low
comedy" touch at the end by reeling off the
stage last of all, quite drunk and leaning
against each other for support; apparently
Borodin's sense of humour was totally un-
sophisticated, not to say simply childish,
though, of course, the inter-mixture of pure
farce with serious drama has plenty of precedents in the works of the greatest of all

dramatists.   Whether the precedents are
worth following is a very different matter and
one which everyone must decide for himself.

The second scene of the act is laid in a
room of Jaroslavna's palace. The princess,
alone, meditates in a long and beautiful
arioso over her loneliness and the fate of her
absent husband as to which she is disturbed
by evil presentiments; the musical handling
of this scene is throughout excellent and as
dramatically true as any number in the opera
—the treatment of the plaintive orchestral
accompaniment being particularly skilful.
The lonely princess is presently interrupted
by her maid (soprano) who introduces the
girls we have seen previously; again they
complain of molestation and beg Jaroslavna's protection and punishment for the
abductor; at first they are afraid to name him
but do so finally, on being urged by the princess, in a striking "allegro vivo" in $\frac{5}{4}$ time,
when Galitsky himself appears, heralded in
the orchestra by a rushing quaver figure
heard in the introduction to his song in scene

one. The girls having fled, a long and dramatic scene follows between brother and sister; Jaroslavna first reproaches and then threatens the dissolute prince with punishment when her husband shall return, to which he replies with contemptuous hints that the latter event is never likely to happen and that she is, indeed, already probably a widow. He goes out to the accompaniment of his leitmotiv (the quaver passage already mentioned) and the unhappy princess is again left alone for a moment, with her anxiety redoubled. Her fears, moreover, are only too well founded for the nobles of the council bring bad news; the army has been surprised and defeated and already the Polovtsi under the terrible Khan Gzak are ravaging the surrounding country; worst of all Igor himself is wounded and with his son a prisoner in the hands of the barbarians. This last news is too much for Jaroslavna; she faints for a moment, then gathering herself together for a final effort appeals to the boyards to protect her and defend the town.

They assure her of their loyalty in a short chorus full of genuine patriotism and affection, but even as all are gathering new hope and courage, the tolling of the alarm-bell is heard, followed by cries of distress from behind the scenes; the Polovtsi have again surprised their foes, and Khan Gzak is already storming the town. The act ends with a scene of wild terror heightened by the really dramatic intensity of the music, pervaded always by the clangour of the alarm-bell; part of the town is already ablaze and the flames throw a lurid glare on the scene in the palace, where the boyards with drawn swords surround their princess—a perfectly natural attitude to adopt in an opera, perhaps, though one cannot help feeling that they could have been better employed elsewhere at such a moment.

In Act II we are transported to the camp of the Polovtsi; it is evening, and Kontchakovna (contralto), daughter of the Khan Kontchak, is amusing herself with the other Polovtsian maidens. The very opening

bars, with their harp chords over a monoton-
ously reiterated A, pizzicato, take us into a
musical atmosphere much more typical of
Borodin than anything we have yet heard;
typical, too, is the lovely, melancholy song
of a solo soprano :

Ex. 23.

with its strange and unforgettable "a piacere" cadenzas; its affinity with a theme,
Ex. 19, from "On the Steppes," has already
been commented on.   The soloist is soon
joined by a chorus of the girls, the monotonous pedal always continuing, and, at the
end, Ex. 23, dies away on the cor anglais.

The next number is a wild "presto" dance

for the girls, often played in the concert-
room with the other dances which conclude
the act.　It is a mad, whirling movement:

Ex. 24.

whose fierce excitement is here and there
whipped up by the mingling of a chromatic
figure in $\frac{5}{8}$ time with the persistent rush of
the $\frac{6}{8}$ rhythm.

A return is now made to the quieter and
more melancholy mood of the opening of
the act; Kontchakovna, softly accompanied
by the chorus, sings a haunting cavatina, full
of florid arabesques and strange Oriental
cadenzas, beautifully echoed by the orchestral wood-wind, in welcome of the gradually-
falling night with its heavy, languorous
atmosphere of love, and softly rejoices that
she will soon see her beloved again.

At the close of her song the Russian prisoners are seen returning under guard from their daily toil, and, at Kontchakovna's bidding, the Polovtsian maidens hasten to offer them food and drink, for which the prisoners express their gratitude in a lovely little "tranquillo" chorus which one can hardly believe is not a genuine folk-song, so simple and natural is its expression. The prisoners again march off, followed by Kontchakovna and the girls; and another piece of naïve beauty ensues when the Polovtsian guard appears, making its round of the camp and singing a quaint refrain :

Ex. 25.

Au sommet des monts le so - leil passe et

By the time it dies away behind the scenes night has fallen, and only the sentinel, Ovlour (tenor), is seen on the stage. Igor's son, Prince Vladimir, now appears and prepares to serenade his captor's daughter, with whom he has fallen in love. Part of his opening recitative may be quoted as an excellent example of Borodin's type of quasi-lyrical declamation (the French version of the words by Madame Alexandrov, being given—as that to which the music is usually sung in Western Europe):

The ensuing cavatina, though the most popular vocal number in the work, is a little too saccharine in sentiment to be altogether pleasing and one always regrets prominence given to any work unworthy of its composer. A fine love-duet between Vladimir and Kontchakovna follows, inspired with real,

sweeping passion, and having a truer ring
of sincerity than many compositions of this
genre which always seem to partake slightly
of artificiality; the orchestral accompaniment, too, with the warm, sweeping arpeggios of the harp, forms an admirable
background, and the whole number is, as it
should be, one of the most outstanding
points in the work. At the end of this ten-
der scene the lovers are interrupted by the
approach of the captive Igor (a striking *ad
lib.* cadenza for the clarinet is noticeable
here), whose great aria, in which he meditates
over his misfortunes, is another of the finest
passages in the opera.

After a sombre recitative passage, introduced by a darkly-coloured orchestral prelude, he breaks into an impassioned
"risoluto":

Ex. 27.

Et puis je vois dans un mi - ra - ge,   Fê - tes, vic-

toi - re, de ja - dis!   etc.

as his rage increases, and he promises himself future vengeance. Then, as his thoughts turn to his absent wife, he sings a quieter, if still passionate melody, warm and flowing:

Ex. 28.

and from these two subjects is woven an aria, which, granted its formal conventionality inherent to the type, is worthy to rank with many of the classic masterpieces in the same form; any lack of vitality in the song as a whole is due entirely to the artificiality of the symmetrical structure as a dramatic medium.

The Polovtsian sentinel Ovlour, who has been converted to Christianity, and hence sympathises with the unfortunate Russians, now approaches Prince Igor and offers to assist his escape; he points to the first tints of dawn, which are just beginning to show themselves,* as a happier omen for Igor and his people, and offers the Prince a fleet horse on which to make his escape. Igor thinks longingly of his unprotected people (the orchestra here recalls the music of the introduction to the Prologue), but finally rejects Ovlour's plan as dishonourable, in spite of the fact that he is bound by no oath, on account of the generosity of his captors and the trust they have shown by allowing him comparative liberty of action.

This kindly attitude of the Polovtsi is further shown on the entrance of the Khan, Kontchak (bass), whose motif :

Ex. 29.

is heard in the orchestra.   He salutes his

---

* A night which only lasts for the duration of three operatic numbers is, of course, even more absurd than the literally "hurricane" eclipse in the Prologue.

prisoner in the kindliest way, bids him raise
his spirits and makes various friendly ad-
vances—the striking progressions of the
diminished fifths* of Ex. 29 being always
prominent in the accompaniment. Then follows a fine aria in which he compliments Igor
on his courage and openly seeks his alliance,
offering him, successively, every gift in his
power, even to the dark beauties of his
harem. Igor, of course, wants nothing but
his freedom, and even this Kontchak willingly offers on condition that the Russians
will not renew the war; the Prince, however,
cannot accede to this, and in a stirring passage, which from mere recitative broadens
out into the pure melody of Ex. 27, affirms
his determination to attempt to avenge his
defeat immediately he is in a position to do
so. The good-humoured Khan, not in the
least angered at the rejection of his amicable
overtures, only praises the invincible spirit

---

* A very similar *motif* based on the same interval plays
an important part in the "storm" music of "Mlada."

and frank speech of his involuntary guest
(his characteristic theme being again to the
fore at this point), for whose amusement he
has prepared a grand divertissement which
concludes the act.

The stage is filled with slaves, male and
female, some carrying tambourines and other
primitive percussion instruments, and then
begins that magnificent series of dances,
familiar to many who have never seen the
opera by reason of the Diaghilev ballet, and
still more, perhaps, on account of numerous
concert-performances. Brilliantly orchestrated by Rimsky-Korsakov, the music is
perfectly effective *per se* without any visual
adjuncts; in conjunction with the scenic
effects and choreography, in which Russian
art is so supremely successful it is overpowering, and one feels that popular opinion
has been right in selecting the Polovtsian
Dances as the most truly representative
pages of the opera.

A short "andantino" prelude gives time
for the gradual entrance of the dancers;

musically it is noticeable for Borodin's employment of his favourite device of a monotonous, throbbing rhythm (continued in the
first dance) on a single note, and for the introduction of a theme :

Ex. 30.

which recurs later in the dances.   First
comes a swaying, undulating dance of girls
who sing, in unison with the oboe, a voluptuous, dreaming melody :

Ex. 31.

accompanied only by the quietly pulsating chords of the harp. Their song is full of languorous sweetness, and tells of the distant summerland of their birth beside the blue, murmuring sea, and its sensuous drowsy movement seems to lull everything into a quiet sleep.

Very different is the next dance, a wild "allegro vivo" for the men. Its sheer naked savagery is dominated throughout by essentially the same rhythm, though now invested with a thoroughly different character, as that which has persisted through the prelude and girls' dance. Even Ex. 30, which is worked a good deal in combination with the chief theme, takes on an air of brutal ferocity.

The chorus is silent throughout this movement, but in the next dance, for the whole company, the full weight of chorus and orchestra is used to produce an overpowering effect of barbaric magnificence:

Ex. 32.

as remarkable a projection of physical ex-
hilaration as the Second Symphony is of
mental exaltation; Rimsky-Korsakov's use of
the percussion instruments, in particular, is
exceedingly brilliant. A temporary relief is
afforded by a sensuous, Orientally-coloured
dance for the female slaves, the music being
identical with that to which Kontchak has

RIMSKY-KORSAKOV.

(By kind permission of M. P. Belaieff, St. Petersburg.)

previously made his offer of any of them to Igor—an offer which he now repeats, after which the gorgeous opulence of Ex. 32 returns again, to die away finally in voluptuous sighs.

Then follows a "presto" boys' dance, stark and fierce, whose mood of savage joy is continued with heightened power in a dance for the men, after which the boys' is repeated—all to music which sounds as astonishingly modern as if it had been written four rather than forty years ago, though little enough that was written in the eighties even *lives* at all to-day.

Next a return is made to the lovely girls' dance, Ex. 31, which is after a time combined with a beautiful variant of the theme of the boys' dance.   After the lovely melody of Ex. 31 has once more wrapped us in its spell of dream-tissue we are brought back to the joys of sheer physical energy in repetitions of the boys' and mens' dances which culminate in a tremendous final choregraphic tableau for the whole company. The music is, at first, based chiefly on the theme of the first "wild dance" of the men, though now clothed in the most resplendent colours of the orchestra, Ex. 30, well to the fore. Gradually the *tempo* becomes more animated, the dance wilder, and the music a sheer riot of blazing sound—a sort of apotheosis of ragtime. Towards the end the senses are overpowered by the blinding brilliance of rhythm and orchestration alike, and when the curtain falls at the end of all the barbaric pageantry one is left with that sense of dizzy intoxication with which only the greatest finales of Wagner and the Seventh Symphony of Beethoven can fill us.

Almost as familiar in the concert-room as the Polovtsian dances is the Polovtsian march, which forms the prelude to the third act of the drama. Another astonishing piece of modernism, its barbaric cruelty is even more marked than that of the dances. Thematically it is chiefly dominated by a striking figure :

Ex. 33.

treated with great ingenuity, the percussion instruments being again used with unerring feeling for effect (by Rimsky-Korsakov—the rest of this third act was completed and scored by Glazounov). Fresh material is soon introduced, though the triplet figure of Ex. 33 is never far in the background, and after a time fanfares of trumpets on the stage behind the curtain are heard.

In the equally fierce Trio two themes of equal importance are employed, one being that previously heard in association with Kontchak—Ex. 29. Towards the end of this section a new fanfare rings out on the trumpets :

Ex. 34.

Marcato

and then the curtain rises on a scene for
which the music has admirably prepared us.
The Polovtsi are swarming from their tents
to greet their triumphant brothers-in-arms,
the warriors of Khan Gzak, who are returning, laden with prisoners and booty, from the
sack of Poutivle. Some of the successful
raiders carry trumpets and tambourines with
which they are celebrating their victory, while
Kontchak's warriors greet their comrades in
a fierce and joyous chorus, which is now combined with the original march-theme. Prince
Igor, Vladimir, and the other Russian prisoners, guessing the meaning of the scene,
watch in mournful silence. The march ends
with a coda, beginning with the materials of
the trio-section but worked up with the
chorus to an overwhelming final climax, during which Khan Gzak himself enters on
horseback with his guards, and is saluted by
Kontchak. The latter welcomes and con-
gratulates him in a very fine and original
aria, in the accompaniment to which his
" leitmotiv," Ex. 29, is, of course, prominent,

punctuated by some tremendous outbursts of full chorus and orchestra—"Glory to the Khans, Gzak and Kontchak."

At the end another great fanfare of trumpets, based on Ex. 34, is heard, and Kontchak, ordering the guards to remove the new prisoners, summons the other Polovtsian chiefs to a grand council in which to discuss plans of future conquest, to which all limits seem to have been removed by this last triumph.

Left to themselves, the unhappy Russians discuss the situation; they are unanimously of the opinion that Igor alone can save his country, and the prince himself perceives that even his personal honour is of less importance than the fate of his fatherland. Even as they are deliberating the extent of the recent disaster is again brought home to them by the arrival, first, of chariots laden with booty, and then of more prisoners, each accompanied by a fresh outburst of the triumphal trumpet-theme, Ex. 34. Finally the stage clears, the Russians having retired to their tents and only the Polovtsian guards remain on duty, while the trumpets sound again in the distance.

There is a chorus for the guards which begins with a reminiscence of their previous song, Ex. 25, and then when Ovlour brings them "koumiss," a drink prepared from fermented mare's milk, which soon intoxicates them, they begin to dance. Once again Borodin finds his truer self when emancipated from verbal fetters, and the music of the dance is as striking, if lacking in the same savage exuberance, as some of the men's dances in the great pageant in the second act. Gradually the effect of the intoxication begins to show itself in another way and, one by one, the dancers drop exhausted to the ground, till finally the whole of the guard is *hors de combat*.

It is now growing dark, and Ovlour, having removed the chief obstacle to his plan, cautiously approaches Igor's tent, while the orchestra quietly gives out the melody in which he first sounded the Prince as to his

willingness to escape. Igor has no longer
any objections, and Ovlour goes off to complete his preparations. But now an unfore-
seen difficulty arises which leads to the real
dramatic climax of the opera. Kontchakovna has by some means discovered
Ovlour's plan, and, alarmed at the prospect
of losing her lover, who is to escape with his
father, endeavours to detain him. She pleads
with him in a fiery, passionate song:

Ex. 35

Allegro appassionato

Tu veux - - - a - vec ton pè - - re, Au

loin por - ter tes pas. etc.

to which Vladimir can only reply by insist-
ing on the call of duty, while Igor, emerging
from his tent, urges his son to delay no
longer. The tense drama of the situation is
admirably, if still conventionally, handled,
and the excitement reaches its height when

Ovlour repeatedly sounds the whistle which
is the prearranged signal for flight.   At last
Kontchakovna in desperation takes the situation into her own hands and sounds the alarm
(the diminished fifths of Ex. 29 being
thundered out in the orchestra).   In the resultant confusion Igor manages to make his
escape with Ovlour, but Vladimir, not perhaps altogether to his distress, is seized by
the furious Polovtsi, and but for Kontchakovna's intervention, seems likely to pay
for his father's liberty with his own life. The
arrival of Kontchak and the other Khans
saves the situation; the good-humoured chief
(for whom Borodin seems to have had more
genuine affection than for his nominal hero)
has only admiration for Igor's daring exploit
and even the traitor Ovlour comes in for no
threats of future punishment.   Still the
other chiefs wish to avenge the flight of their
principal captive by a massacre of the other
prisoners, but the Khan is firm and drastic-
ally settles the problem of Vladimir's future
by giving him his daughter in marriage—the

strongest tie, as he tells the others, by which he could possibly hold him captive. Once again the Polovtsi prepare for war; their fierce barbaric choruses in honour of their chiefs end with a tremendous downward-rushing chromatic scale in the orchestra, and then, after the fall of the curtain, the trumpets sound for the last time their great challenge, Ex. 34. In the fourth, and last, act, we return to Poutivle; the scene is laid in the great square of the town, at daybreak, and Jaroslavna is seen alone on the top of the battlements. Her lament, a most typical melody of melancholy beauty, is echoed by the orchestra with an effect as exquisite as that of the Shepherd Scene of "Tristan." Once or twice the second subject of Igor's aria in Act II, Ex. 28, is introduced, with the never-failing effect produced by the leit-motiv when used with such moderation, and from this and other material is woven some of the most genuinely beautiful pages of the whole score.

As her song concludes and she is left alone

with her thoughts, an interlude, typically
naïve in its nature but amply justified by its
simple perfection of beauty, occurs.   The
voices of a party of villagers are heard
gradually approaching; their song, almost
unaccompanied throughout, is of the ravages
of the war and the miseries brought in the
train of the all-conquering Gzak, but the
music must rank among the most beautiful
that Borodin or any other Russian composer,
has ever written.   First only a solo soprano
is heard :

Ex. 36.

and then the other female voices (in four
parts) take up the strain. As the peasants
cross the stage, the male voices are added,
and then when the party disappears their
voices are heard for some time gradually re-

ceding in the distance—the same hackneyed device that Borodin has also employed in the "Steppenskizze" yet somehow transfigured by his magic touch and treatment into an effect of inexpressible loveliness. The subject of the song only serves, of course, to plunge Jaroslavna into deeper gloom, but suddenly her attention is attracted by two objects in the distance. She makes out the figures of two horsemen, and recognises the dress of one of them as that of a Polovtsian warrior—a threat of new terrors; but the other she perceives is a Russian, an idea flashes into her mind (Borodin's direction at this point is most illuminating—"with great emotion and *almost* declaimed," though the whole of this part of her music has been undeniable recitative) can it be? it *is* her Igor!

The Prince appears, dismounts and rushes to embrace his wife, while Ovlour tactfully withdraws with the horses. A long and rapturous duet follows, as a matter of course, at the end of which they walk slowly in the

direction of the citadel before which they
stop for a few moments, deep in their conversation.

Now comes another humorous episode,
provided by the two goudok-players,
Eroschka and Skoula; these two heroes, the
music of whose instruments is suggested by
a four note ostinato semiquaver figure in the
orchestra, enter and begin a long song in
derision of this noble fool, Prince Igor,
whose heroics have come to such a dismal
conclusion. They are still making merry at
his expense when, to their horror, they discover that the subject of their jests is not
only at liberty once more but actually within
earshot. Fortunately for their skins, however, he and Jaroslavna have been so absorbed in their conversation that they have
heard nothing, and indeed, presently disappear into the citadel. Still the situation
is, for the unhappy musicians, fairly desper-
ate; their share in Galitsky's treason is well-
known, and Eroschka, taking a gloomy view
of things, predicts hanging as their inevit-

able fate. Skoula, not so easily discouraged, refuses to give up hope yet, and, after rejecting flight as an equally unpleasant alternative, devises a plan which for its impudence certainly deserves the success it attains. The music of this scene, it may be said, is as successful in its portrayal of humour as music possibly can be; its material is mainly derived from the four-note "goudok"-theme. Briefly Skoula's plan is to secure forgiveness for past offences by being the first to demonstrate their loyalty on their Prince's return; to this end both begin a furious clamour on the alarm-bells and call the townspeople together. Owing to their mysteriously important method of making their announcement the crowd is at first under the impression that they are either drunk or playing a practical joke, but the facts are made clear at last, to the great joy of the people, and soon the nobles and other officials, having heard the rumour, appear on the scene. The latter look upon the goudok-players with suspicion and accuse them of having been in

the service of Galitsky, a calumnious insin-
uation which they immediately and scorn-
fully repudiate; they are far too honest, and
as for their loyalty have they not just given
ample proof of it?   Such services as theirs,
they think, are worthy of reward, and, rather
to their surprise, they get it.

The concluding number is a broad chorus,
"allegro marziale":

Ex. 37.

led by the two rascals, in praise of the Prince.
Gradually the crowd increases, some of the
newcomers bearing bread and salt, the tra-

ditional symbols of welcome, till at last Igor
emerges from the Kremlin, with Jaroslavna
and his nobles, and is received with overwhelming shouts of joy.   The last broad and
dignified page of the chorus, "maestoso and
tranquillo," shows real depth of sincerity and
affection, and rings more true than any of the
musically rather spurious enthusiasm which
has preceded it.

As has already been mentioned, the overture to "Prince Igor" is based entirely on
themes taken from the body of the work and
derives a special interest from the fact that,
having never been written out by Borodin,
it was reproduced from memory and orchestrated by Glazounov, who had often heard
the composer play it on the piano.   Unlike
the average modern operatic overture, it
makes no impossible attempt to sketch the
outline of the plot beforehand nor even,
somewhat unfortunately, to create an atmosphere.   As it is, the overture is quite a strong
and virile piece of work—fiery, energetic and
curiously full of indications of the direct

influence of Glinka (cf. the latter's overture to "A Life for the Czar," for instance). An "andante" introduction of thirty-nine bars is based chiefly on the prelude to Igor's aria in Act II; later the quiet progression of chords, associated in the Prologue with the ladies, is heard and then the "allegro" (in D major) opens with an extended version of the "fanfare" theme, Ex. 34. This is immediately worked up to a tremendous climax in which the tumultuous passages of Igor's and Jaroslavna's duet of re-union in the last act burst forth. Next comes Kontchakovna's song from Act III, Ex. 35, followed by the diminished fifths of Ex. 29, and the rest of the material for the exposition section is provided by Exs. 27 and 28 from Igor's great aria in the second act. The latter, especially, is treated at considerable length and with great beauty; as it dies away the quiet chord-progression is heard and then the development begins with a lengthy treatment of Ex. 35 on the 'cellos and basses. Ex. 34 is next re-introduced and cleverly interwoven with

the Igor-Jaroslavna duet theme; this in turn
is followed by a long passage identical with
that which, in the opera, accompanies Kontchak's introductory recitative to his air in
Act II. The recapitulatory section is followed by a coda in which Exs. 28 and 35 are
cleverly combined simultaneously and the
whole whipped up into a climax of fiery brilliance; the final "animato" being practically
identical with the conclusion of the third act
of the opera. Effective though it be, in its
capable symphonic handling of the material,
as a concert-piece, one cannot help wishing
that Borodin, had he lived, would have dis-
placed this overture in favour of some form
of prelude more calculated to prepare the
listener for the general atmosphere of the
work, to put him in a sympathetic, and therefore receptive, frame of mind, and to "set
the stage" generally.

The dramatic faults of "Prince Igor"
have already been touched on and, on this
head, there is little more to be said. Above
all the play, as a play, is so hopelessly inde-

9

finite. Wagner sometimes went to the other extreme of leaving nothing to the imagination and filling in and underlining every point of detail or subtlety; Borodin, on the other hand, in his very proper endeavour to work only in broad outlines becomes hopelessly vague. We want to know what has happened to the villain of the piece, Galitsky, who, after assuming great temporary importance at the beginning, inconsequently disappears after his scene with his sister and is scarcely alluded to afterwards. We are quite rightly left to draw our own conclusions as to what happened at the partial sack of Poutivle (Wagner would have devoted at least a quarter of an hour to a detailed narration of its incidents) and as to Vladimir's fate—obviously a happy one—but the final situation is scarcely a satisfactory or conclusive one. At the end of Act III the Polovtsi are preparing to renew the war and now we see Igor proposing to try to chastise them again (the same situation as that with which the opera opens) and with that knowledge we have to be content, but it certainly seems a grave fault of construction to cut short the action at this particular point. An even more serious defect than this or than the absurd ten-minute-night in Act II is the failure of the characters to show any but the faintest signs of coming to life. Igor, Vladimir and Galitsky are all mere lay-figures; Kontchakovna, passionate as she is supposed to be, is little more. One would like to believe in the good-natured Khan, her father, who would have made a decidedly more attractive hero than Igor, but he is scarcely more than sketched. Ovlour, another dummy, for whom we are supposed to have sympathetic feelings, seems a rather despicable traitor (indeed, the Christians show up rather badly throughout, in comparison with the pagan Polovtsi). Jaroslavna alone of all the characters lives and breathes—and she is off the stage for two whole acts.

It is on the strength of its music alone that "Prince Igor" will live, and even that is unequal. Broadly speaking, the music of the second and third acts belongs to quite another plane to that of the rest of the opera. The Oriental atmosphere of these scenes produced in Borodin a reaction which led to the creation of some of his finest and most characteristic music—music which has not even yet lost the fresh tang of modernity—but, despite some fine moments, the bulk of the rest of the work scarcely shows the composer at anything more than his second-best.

This employment of the leitmotiv is nearly always effective, though one is inclined to attribute its rather frequent use in the third act to the hand of Glazounov, who would naturally have wished to confine himself as much as possible to Borodin's own thematic material, but his usual moderation is productive of really more striking stage-results than Wagner's over-elaborated system which often resulted in loss of dramatic significance to individual themes through too much repetition.

Borodin's compromise on melodic recitative can only be regarded as partially successful *in his own hands*, yet one feels that he was probably on the right track and that, used *consistently* without lapses into formal, balanced melody, his method is the best medium of musico-dramatic expression. Our own British national opera, if we are ever to have one, will never be based on Wagnerian methods and this experiment of a Russian composer, inconclusive though it be, should be of value to any modern Englishman in a similar predicament.* To sum up; "Prince Igor" was intended to be a dramatic work, and, as a drama, despite a very great deal of remarkably fine music, it is a comparative failure—a colossal failure, it is true, one of those failures which are worth more than many triumphs, but still a failure. Regarded as a musical work, pure and simple, despite

---

* Mr. Rutland Boughton has worked on not dissimilar lines to Borodin in this respect, but he clings too tightly to the leitmotiv.

its weaknesses, it is a genuine masterpiece,
and, though not one great coherent whole,
its parts are generally fine, lucid and vital,
while not a few are touched with deathless
beauty.

IV.—THE CHAMBER-MUSIC.

WE have already noticed that one of the chief (if not the chief) characteristics of Borodin's music, in common with that of most Russians, is a striving after brilliant, if sometimes crude, impressions of colour—a striving which led him to the creation of new and remarkable effects of orchestration. It would seem, then, that chamber-music, the form of music which allows less scope than any other for brilliance, colour or any other type of superficiality of appeal, would have proved to Borodin a most uncongenial medium of expression, yet, like Tchaïkovsky, who actually expressed his antipathy for it, he was able to use it with the greatest success.

It is true that his output of chamber-music was not large—two full-sized string quartets and two separate movements for the same combination, all written toward the end of his life—but it is none the less characteristic. Musical "colour" is a term rather loosely applied to two quite different means of obtaining contrasts of tonal effect, the orchestral, produced by combinations of instruments of different timbre, and another, which is the result of both harmonic effects and exploitation of the different qualities of tone obtainable from instruments of the same timbre, and which is more akin to the nuances of tone in a monochrome painting than to actual colour. When deprived of the first means Borodin availed himself to the full of the second, with the result that his chamber-music is, in its way, as much marked by novelty of effect as is anything he wrote. He even denied himself such advantages of novelty as other modern composers have derived from the introduction of wind-instruments into this sphere, while the combination of piano with strings was probably as unpleasant to him as to Tchaïkovsky.

The First String Quartet,* in A major, is dedicated to the wife of his friend, Rimsky-Korsakov, herself a talented musician, and, as the composer informs us on the title-page, was largely inspired by a theme from Beethoven's Quartet in B flat, Op. 139.† This latter point is the more interesting because, as is well-known, the great German master had been an admirer of Russian folk-songs and had used them in some of his own chamber-works, notably the first two Rasumovsky Quartets (Op. 59, Nos. 1 and 2). One feels Borodin's action as the delicate returning of an international compliment. The actual music, however, shows comparatively little trace of Teutonic influence.

The First Quartet opens with a very beautiful and tranquil "moderato" introduction:

* Composed about 1877-8.
Itself dedicated to a Russian—Prince Nicholas Galitsin.

Ex. 38.

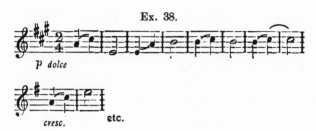

in which the figures of the first four bars are much used. This leads, through a twelve-bar accelerando, to a light-hearted "allegro," much of it quite full of a quite idyllic contentment and clarity of thought. The first subject falls into two main parts* :

Ex. 39.

---

* The derivation of Ex. 39 from Beethoven's :

Ex. 39a.

is quite obvious.

and :

Ex. 40.

both entrusted to the first violin and, after a
time, handed on to the second and then to
the 'cello.   An episode entirely built up of a
short, but important, subsidiary *motif* :

Ex. 41.

reaches a passionate climax and leads to a
deeply-moved, rather Chopinesque, second
subject, "espressivo ed appassionato " :

Ex. 42.

the sequential nature of which betrays a
Western influence rather foreign to Borodin.

Its gloomy passion is intensified when it reappears on the dark lower register of the
viola.

The development begins with a quiet and
rather mysterious treatment of Ex. 41, the
effect being coloured and intensified by the
use of 'cello harmonics, and the whole of this
section is carried out with the greatest contrapuntal skill—fragments of Exs. 39, 40,
41 and 42 being worked together with an ingenuity which reminds one of Wagner's
famous combinations of themes in the
" Meistersinger " overture and the Finale of
" Die Walküre."

Then Ex. 40 is worked alone in a vigorous
" fugato " passage of some length which cul-
minates in a very characteristic treatment of
Ex. 41 on viola and 'cello (the first five
quavers broken up into semiquavers) and
punctuated by sforzando chords on the violins—an effect belonging to the realm of the
orchestra rather than to that of chamber-
music, but none the less striking.

A return is next made to the theme of the

introduction, Ex. 38, on the violins, "dolce
cantabile," while viola and 'cello alternately
meditate over Ex. 41. The development
concludes with a return to Ex. 42 accompanied by arpeggio figures in cross-rhythms
on viola and 'cello.

The recapitulation follows, on the usual
lines, without any very radical difference in
the manner of presentation of the subject-
matter, and concludes with a fairly lengthy
coda in which Ex. 41 and the fifth and sixth
bars of Ex. 40 form the chief thematic
material. The long trills for first violin, re-
minding one distantly of the orchestral
"Steppenskizze," are very characteristic, and
the soaring passages for first violin and viola
with the ethereal close are particularly beautiful. In the lyrical slow movement, "andante con moto," contrapuntal interest again
plays an important part. The movement
opens with two themes of equal importance,
in invertible counterpoint, on the first violin
and viola :

Ex. 43.

This mood of quiet contemplation is suddenly interrupted by a passionate *ff* cry,
"energico ed appassionato," from the first
violin, a descending passage in triplets, into
which, were one so inclined, it would not be
difficult to read some programmatic significance.   In such cases, however, it is always
well to ignore such extra-musical suggestions
and judge the music for *itself* and on its
merits as purely abstract music; by so doing
we shall avoid falling into the fantastic and
ridiculous extravagances of Berlioz and
others who have sought to illuminate the im-
aginary obscurities of Beethoven by the light
of their own too fertile imaginations.

The more lyrical mood is immediately resumed with a new and apparently rather
unimportant subject :

Ex. 44.

p cantabile   etc.

of a more flowing character, with a chromatic
pendant :

Ex. 45.

which assumes considerable importance and
colours the whole movement with an almost
Tchaïkovskian gloom. From this last theme
is constructed a mysterious "fugato" middle
section, at the close of which the passionate
violin interruption again appears with an
almost hysterical intensity caused by the
highest register of the instrument to which
it is now given. Ex. 43 now returns, first
in its original form, and then, after a few
bars, inverted—the upper theme now on

viola and 'cello in octaves and the lower on
the violins (also in octaves)—*ff* "marcato."
The "appassionato" triplet passage intrudes
for the third and last time, in the deeper and
richer tones of the viola and 'cello, and this
curiously enigmatic movement concludes,
after final references to Ex. 45, over a throbbing tonic pedal on the 'cello, with the chord
of the tonic major (F sharp), which dies
away *pppp*.

The "prestissimo" Scherzo, in F natural,
is a sparkling, elfish movement like that of
the First Symphony, a little reminiscent of
some of Beethoven's scherzi or of Berlioz's
celebrated "Queen Mab" movement in
"Romeo and Juliet," and therefore not very
typical either of Borodin or of Russian music
in general. Thematically, it is dominated
by a little three-note motif:

Ex. 46.

M. A. BALAKIREV.

(By permission of M. P. Belaieff, St. Petersburg.)

p. 123.

which is tossed lightly from one instrument
to another in delicate, flitting figures and is
later used as a sort of basso ostinato to a
more extended theme of very similar
character.

The Trio, a "moderato," in $\frac{2}{4}$ time, is more
characteristic and affords an excellent illus-
tration of the varieties of timbre which Borodin could obtain from the strings alone. The
viola, muted, plays a rather sombre little
tune to a running accompaniment of semiquavers on the second violin, also muted,
while 'cello and first violin colour the whole
with their silvery harmonics—an effect which
was then unique in the literature of chamber-
music and foreshadowed some of the most
interesting developments of the Impressionist school in this direction. The repetition
of the scherzo follows according to the classical models. The Finale is introduced by
twenty-six bars of "andante" brooding over
Ex. 44 previously heard in the slow movement, now in A minor, and whose signifi-

cance is now fully revealed.*   Three *sfor-*
zando chords herald the forceful "allegro
risoluto," which, like the slow movement,
opens at once with two equally important
subjects in double counterpoint.   The viola
has a staccato version of Ex. 44 against
which the first violin plays a striking theme,
"risoluto ed energico":

Ex. 47.

and from these two, with a rather unimportant second subject:

Ex. 48.

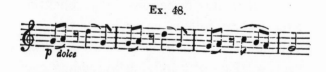

---

* Its affinity with Ex. 39 shows it to have been conceived as a variant of the Beethoven "motto-theme."

the whole of the thematic material is derived.
Exs. 44 and 47 appear almost always in combination both in a "più animato" codetta
to the exposition section, the whole of which
is repeated, and in much of the development.
In this another display of contrapuntal skill
is given, Ex. 48 being not only used as a
bass to a new theme but also worked in counterpoint with Ex. 47. It must be understood, however, that there is nothing of the
pedantic in the music, for the whole movement is as healthy and invigorating as a stiff
sea-breeze, and one always feels that the
technical ingenuity, though not quite natural
to the composer's temperament, is merely
the means to an end and never the end itself.

The recapitulation is perfectly orthodox,
and with the return of the second subject,
Ex. 48, we again reach the central key of the
quartet—A major. In the coda, marked by
a continual increasing of the pace, Ex. 44
reigns supreme, and the work concludes with
a brilliant effect, obtained by writing for all
four instruments in their highest possible

register, which really needs an orchestra to make it effective. Regarded as a whole, the quartet, while scarcely a masterpiece, is a most interesting and homogeneous piece of work, worthy of much more frequent performance than has yet been accorded it, though from the emotional and purely æsthetic point of view, it is far inferior to the first three movements of its less-sophisticated successor in D major.

This latter work, dedicated to Madame Borodin, is unsurpassed in sheer lyrical beauty by anything the composer wrote. In it all technical ingenuity is entirely subordinated to pure beauty, the mere formal structure (perfect as it is—perhaps because of its perfection) is so natural that it is quite unheeded, and the effects of "colour," numerous and lovely as they are, seem to spring naturally from the music (largely from the crystal clarity of the harmony) rather than to be introduced for their own sake, as in the Trio of the First Quartet.

The first movement, a stream of uninter-

rupted loveliness, opens "allegro moderato," without the least preamble, with a
beautiful tune, on the cello:

Ex. 49.

which is immediately taken up by the first
violin. After a time another, even more
typically Slavonic, theme:

Ex. 50.

which is related to the continuation of Ex.
49, appears on the first violin with a pizzicato accompaniment. A third subject, which
need not be quoted, completes the thematic
material of the movement, which is not only
shorter, but in every way simpler, than the
corresponding movement in the First Quartet. The exposition closes with a charming
little codetta, based on a chromatic descend-

ing figure of four notes, and the short development follows—marked by no contrapuntal *tours de force*, but full of the limpid
sweetness which is felt in every bar of the
quartet and delightful harmonies and modu-
lations which suggest the untroubled spirit
of a Schubert or a Dvorák.   In the recapitulation Ex. 50 is given to the viola, the 'cello
accompaniment foreshadowing Stravinsky's
treatment of that instrument, and afterwards
with particularly beautiful effect to the first
violin and 'cello in octaves.   At the end the
little chromatic figure, before referred to,
again appears in a lengthy coda whose dying
echoes are the inevitable epilogue to the
poetry which has preceded it.

In happy contrast comes the light-hearted
Scherzo, here placed before the slow movement which approximates too nearly to the
feeling of the first movement to provide an
adequate contrast to it.   This scherzo, of a
totally different character to the other and
far more individual is predominated by a

light tripping "allegretto" figure on the
violins:

Ex. 51.

which is succeeded, after a time, by a more
sustained melody in thirds (meno mosso),
also given to the violins, while the 'cello has
an accompaniment of broken chords of a
type similar to that mentioned in the preceding movement; after a time Ex. 51 reappears on the viola as a sort of undercur-
rent to the more suave second subject.
Instead of a Trio section there is a regular
development (for the movement, slight
though its material, is in full sonata-form)
chiefly based on Ex. 51, though fresh matter is introduced. After the recapitulation
comes a coda of delightful piquancy, which,
after working up to a brilliant "vivace,"
closes quietly with a few bars of unexpected
grace and delicacy.

The ensuing Nocturne is, justly, the most
popular individual movement of Borodin's
chamber-music; he certainly never wrote
anything more thoroughly characteristic.
The beautiful 'cello melody:

Ex. 52.

cast in the same mould as Ex. 19, from "On
the Steppes," with its throbbing syncopated
accompaniment on second violin and viola,
plunges us at once into the heavy, languorous atmosphere of a summer night in Russia
—an atmosphere quite Oriental in its sensuous relaxation and one which seems to have
had an extraordinary fascination for Russian musicians, from Rimsky-Korsakov (in

his " Nuit de Mai ") to Stravinsky, whose
" L'Oiseau de Feu " is full of it.   After a
time the first violin takes up the melody (as
if one heavy perfume had melted imper-
ceptibly into another) like a distant voice
full of subdued passion.   Later the passion
seems to break its bonds, in a long " più
mosso " section built up from a new theme
with a modal touch in its tonality, a forceful
two-octave scale, " appassionato e risoluto,'
culminating in repetitions of an emphatic
little figure equally impassioned in character; yet, through it all, Ex. 52 winds its way,
now on one instrument, now on another, like
a singer unconscious of the passions she is
arousing in her hearers.   At the return of
the first *tempo* a lovely effect is created by
the first violin echoing the 'cello melody, *pp*,
in canon, at the distance of one beat; then
when the first violin takes up the tune the
second has the echo—another instance of
technical skill, though only a pedant would
think of it as such.   The " risoluto " scale-
passage reappears once or twice, but so

altered in character as to suggest confidence
rather than passionate questioning. As the
movement draws to an end it seems to fade
out in distance, its dying echoes, in which
the seventh bar of Ex. 52 passes from one
instrument to another again and again, as if
they are loth to leave it, haunting the ear,
seem when they finally vanish to leave us
with that sense of emptiness which comes
when something extremely beautiful is suddenly snatched from us. The Finale, attractive and vivacious as it is, is scarcely on
the same level as the three preceding movements. Why, it is difficult to say—for one
can bring no very definite positive charge
against it. To borrow Reynolds's famous
phrase, "it lacks *that*." The short "andante" introduction is concerned with the
alternate presentation of two themes:

Ex. 53.

on the violins, and ;

Ex. 54.

on viola and 'cello. Then, "vivace," the
'cello leads off a lively dance with Ex. 54,
and the viola, second violin and first violin
in succession take up Ex. 53, Ex. 54 being
always treated as a counter-subject. The
real "second subject" is somewhat quieter
in mood, but the music dances on its way as
light-heartedly as a Haydn movement, the
only interruption occurring at the beginning
of the development and recapitulation sec-
tions, when the brief introductory passage
reappears—Ex. 54 sounding in graver tones,
while Ex. 53, still in the quicker *tempo*,
seems impatient to get back to the vivacious
dance. The final climax, brilliant as it is,
never oversteps the bounds of chamber-
music and well rounds off a work which deserves to rank among the finest quartets of
the post-Beethoven period of the last cen-

tury. Borodin's other contributions to the
chamber-music literature are comparatively
unimportant. One forms part of one of
those collective efforts, like "Mlada," whose
title-pages suggest the work of a syndicate
—a quartet on the name "B-la-f," in which
his collaborators were Rimsky-Korsakov,
Liadov and Glazounov.

Mitrophone Petrovitch Belaïeff, a keen
musical amateur and admirer of the nationalist school, having amassed a large fortune
in his business as timber-merchant, was able
to show his sympathy with the movement in
a practical way, and, in 1885, founded the
famous publishing house which bears his
name and which has done incalculable good
to the cause of Russian music by bringing
out works by young and unknown composers
which would otherwise have been con-
demned (from financial considerations) to
remain in manuscript—unplayed and un-
heard. To this Mæcenas the four composers above-mentioned, by a happy inspiration, agreed to pay a tribute of homage and

gratitude by writing a quartet in which the
theme of each movement should be based
on the musical equivalent of his name,
B-la-f—B being the German name for B flat
and la the French for A.* Rimsky-Korsakov wrote the first movement, Liadov the
second—a rather Beethovenian scherzo,
with a lovely, haunting folk-song-like trio—
and Glazounov the brilliant finale. Borodin's contribution was the very short third
movement—a " Serenata alla spagnola," the
only instance of his succumbing to the curious Russian mania for quasi-Spanish atmosphere, started by Glinka in his "Caprice
Brillant" and "Souvenir d'une nuit d'été à
Madrid," and which reached its high-water
mark of musical excellence in Rimsky-Korsakov's brilliant, if superficial, "Capriccio
Espagnol." The B-la-f theme appears first
in some introductory chords for violins and

---

* Alexander Kopylov has used the same theme in his
Andantino, Op. 7, and a Prelude and Fugue, Op. 11—
both for string quartet—and so has Sokolov in his Serenade, Op. 3.

'cello, pizzicato, which then form the accompaniment to a viola melody :

Ex. 55.

cantabile con espressione

B - - la - - f   B - - la - - f

There is a livelier middle section, in which the Spanish element is suggested by characteristic rhythms, and then a repetition of the first part. At the end, "più lento," the viola sighs out the last three notes of Ex. 55, "con dolore e lamentoso," finishing with a curious little cadenza on the same *motif*.

Borodin also contributed a transcription of the Scherzo in D major, from the unfinished Third Symphony, to the second volume of "Les Vendredis"—a collection of short, "recreation" pieces for string quartet, by various composers, published by Belaïeff—in which form it is only moderately successful. Owing to its original purpose it is, of course, longer than most of the other pieces in the collection and the other scherzi

in his own quartets, and one feels that its
thematic material is of too slight nature to
provide the substance of a monochromatic
movement of such dimensions.   The lovely
Trio, being less dependent on orchestral
colour for its success, retains its attractions
in this medium, and one would willingly
hear the whole Scherzo for its sake alone,
the more so as opportunities of making its
acquaintance in the orchestral form are
practically nil.   However it would be mani-
festly unfair to condemn the Scherzo
because it is a comparative failure as chamber-music, for it must be remembered that
no genuinely orchestral movement could be
anything else.

V.—MISCELLANEOUS
COMPOSITIONS.

THE study of a composer's smaller compositions is always an interesting, sometimes a vastly illuminating process. In such works one is often able to catch the composer's mind off its guard, so to speak, and to surprise the most intimate revelations—thoughts and facets of mentality of the existence of which one would otherwise never suspect. This is the case not merely with men like Chopin and Scriabin, who have actually excelled in the miniature-form, who have encased their best work in its tiny shell, but with those, such as Elgar or even Beethoven himself, to whom the writing of small-scale works has meant little more than an artistic form of pot-boiling. However much a composer may have his tongue in his cheek he is none the less expressing a part of himself; the unworthiest part, certainly, but still a mental phase, and perhaps we do wrong to neglect the importance of *pièces d'occasion* and the like in estimating the mental composition of any creative artist, be he poet or musician. It is, of course, customary to slur over a work like Beethoven's "Battle of Vittoria" as a mere mental aberration; so it may have been, but in conjunction with the "Pastoral" Symphony, it throws a sidelight on an interesting phase, if a regrettable one, of Beethoven's character—as, in another way, does the "Grosse Fuge." Musically, such works are quite negligible; psychologically they are invaluable.

In Borodin's case there was, of course, no necessity for musical "pot-boiling." Music was for him simply a hobby, and although he was not particularly wealthy his profes-

11

sional income was always sufficient to place
him beyond the need of augmenting it to
any great extent. He was therefore never
under the necessity of creating, or at least
publishing, anything which did not entirely
satisfy his own standards of critical require-
ment. On only one occasion was he asked
to produce anything "to order," and then,
as we have seen, he acquitted himself remarkably well. The weakness of his
smaller works is just this—that they are obviously the result of odd moments. Borodin, like most Russians (Scriabin is the only
really important exception), thought greatly
and on broad lines, and he needed a large
framework on which to extend his ideas.
The miniature form and still more the limi-
tations of the piano-keyboard and tone-
colour, so much more cramping than those of
the string quartet, gave him little scope to
develop the more commonplace odds and
ends of thoughts which were relegated to
this medium, and moreover the intimacy of

the type sometimes betrayed him into a mood of sentimentality of which his larger works show no sign.

These few short miscellaneous works fall almost entirely into two categories—piano-music and songs, neither of great bulk. His achievements in the realm of solo piano-music are all summed-up in the well-known collection of short *salon* pieces, the " Petite Suite "—one of his later productions, being written about 1885 and dedicated to his friend, the Belgian countess. None of the members of the " Invincible Band " were particularly successful as piano-composers, Cui, perhaps, the most. Balakirev, judging by his " Islamey " fantasia and his reputation as a performer, might have done great things,* but Moussorgsky's keyboard-works are thoroughly un-pianistic while Rimsky-Korsakov's small output is most uninteresting. Borodin has never in the " Petite

---

* His Sonata in B minor is never heard in England, but is probably very interesting.

Suite" overstepped the bounds of true
piano-music and has, further, produced a
set of little pieces whose moods, while having little in common with those most truly
typical of the composer, are not without a
tinge of a certain attractive charm of their
own. Their influence, too, on the *salon*
works of later Russian musicians has not
been inconsiderable. The first number, at
once the best and the most popular of all
Borodin's smaller works, is the now almost
hackneyed "Au Couvent"—a short impression informed with real beauty and affording
splendid opportunities for variations of
piano tone-quality to the discerning pianist.
The opening :

Ex. 56.

with its clever suggestion of bells by the use
of overtones, is an example of an effect for
which most Russian composers have had an
affection; Rimsky-Korsakov employed it in
his opera, "The Maid of Pskov," and Moussorgsky has introduced it in "Boris
Godounov," the well-known prelude to his
"Khovantchina" and the "Exhibition Pictures" for piano.   Fortunately Borodin has
managed to avoid any suggestion of the pictorial "cheapness" with which such methods
are too often associated, and the solemn tolling prepares the mind accurately for the
mood-picture which it introduces.   The real
thematic basis of the piece is a tranquil
melody of obviously liturgical associations:

Ex. 57.

p dolce e con simplicita   (L.H.)

etc.

stated at first unaccompanied and with the
utmost simplicity.   Gradually its treatment
becomes broader and more sonorous, till it

piles up at its climax into an almost organ-
like grandeur of massive tone. The theme
is then heard again more quietly, finally
dying away and the piece ends with a return
to Ex. 56.

The second number is an Intermezzo in
F—a rather commonplace "Tempo di
Minuetto," as square and colourless as early
Grieg and lacking both the graceful charm
of the old minuet and the playful vivacity of
the newer type. The middle section, "un
poco meno mosso":

Ex. 58.

is more attractive and particularly interesting
for its foreshadowing, in both manner and
substance, of much of Scriabin's earlier
work, especially at the period (about Op. 11
to 17) when he was beginning to emanci-
pate himself from Chopinesque mannerism
and formulate a more definitely personal
style of utterance. Borodin is not usually
considered among those from whom Scriabin derived in any way but there are, none
the less, grounds for supposing that the
latter was influenced to a certain extent by
other numbers of the "Petite Suite"—the
two Mazurkas and the "Rêverie," for instance. No. 3 of the Suite is a vivacious
Mazurka in C, full of attractive high spirits
but not of much importance. In thinking
of mazurkas a comparison with Chopin is
almost inevitable, but, in this instance, the
influence of the Polish composer is nowhere
apparent; the second subject in G might be
taken from one of the lighter pages of Moussorgsky's "Boris."   There is a short "meno

mosso" middle section in E flat and a final coda tinged with sly humour.

No. 4 is another Mazurka (in D flat) but quite different in character from the preceding one. Its chief subject, a warm "cantabile espressivo ed amoroso" melody for the left-hand, beautiful as it is, is slightly reminiscent of Chopin, and indeed the whole piece is entirely pervaded with Chopinesque sentiment and mannerisms. As in the companion piece there is a short trio after which the first section is repeated.

The succeeding "Rêverie," in D flat, is a brief page, recalling in its sentimentality the "Consolations" of Franz Liszt (whose influence is also, but more slightly, apparent in "Au Couvent"). It has also a certain curious affinity with the more mawkish moods of Edward Macdowell and, of course, with the younger Scriabin; such sickly self-communings seem quite foreign to Borodin, whose day-dreams are almost always felt and expressed with real sincerity. The vein of rather saccharine charm which character-

ises the "Rêverie" is again present in the
two succeeding numbers, which conclude the
suite, though in a more attractive disguise.
The "Serenade" is, as its title demands,
pervaded with a heavy amorous perfume
akin to that with which Rachmaninov's
shorter works have familiarised us. The
prevailing rhythm, a quiet rocking figure, is
first presented in a few introductory bars
and then used as the accompaniment to a
quaint "amoroso" melody, piquantly accentuated, in the full, rich middle register of
the instrument. The music gradually becomes more passionate in its warmth and
then dies down in a passage like a succession of gentle sighs. A last pp reference
to the opening bars with their tranquil
rhythmic pulse brings the piece to an end.

In the concluding "Nocturne" the atmosphere is again dark, thick, sensuous and
heavily oppressive. The mood and substance of the piece are, as before, hinted at
in three preludial bars and then emerge in
full as :

Ex. 59.

the monotonous reiterated quavers being present throughout. The coda is marked by a poetic little touch, the introduction of an entirely new melody, "marcato assai, amoroso, espressivo," in the tenor register, for the left hand, while the right hand continues the figure of Ex. 59. The new melody introduces a note of reassurance and repose, and in this mood the piece closes, although the reiterated B flats of Ex. 59 are sounded *ppp*, a little wistfully, at the end.

It will be noticed that the Suite has no organic existence as a whole, and is merely a collection of quite independent pieces without any more relation or connection than that given them by the caprice of the composer in issuing them together. Their technical demands are so comparatively modest as to place them well within the reach of any quite moderately gifted amateur, but it would be misleading him to suggest that they are in any way genuinely representative of their composer's genius.

The only other compositions of Borodin's for the piano that one ever meets with are his contributions to the humorously conceived collection of short pieces for piano-duet known as "Paraphrases" by various members of the "Kouchka" and their ally Liadov. The idea of writing a piano-duet in which one player has only a "chopsticks" part while the other provides the real musical interest is said to have been suggested to Borodin by one of his adopted daughters who was unable to play the piano yet wished to participate in a small way in the delights of actual musical performance. The *bizarrerie* of the notion caught the fancy of Borodin and his friends, who, as the result, produced (about 1877) a collection of little pieces based on this idea, the whole set being dedicated "to little pianists capable of performing the theme with one finger of each hand." Cui, Liadov and Rimsky-Korsakov joined in the composition of twenty-four variations with a finale, on the theme, and the rest of the work consisted of fourteen short independent pieces by Borodin and the three aforementioned composers; after Borodin's death another number of his, a mazurka, was added, while another supplementary piece, "Bigarrures," was later appended by N. V. Stcherbatchev, a young ally of the "Band."

It cannot be claimed that either of Borodin's four contributions has any musical value, and, indeed, their interest is entirely dependent on the curious device to which they owe their inception and on the com-

poser's ingenious handling of it.   The first
number is an amusing "vivo" "Polka," the
squareness of the rhythm of this dance being
admirably suited to the theme :

Ex. 60.

which, as in all the pieces, provides an incessant "ostinato" upper part. To this
"Polka" Liszt, as a playful little token of
his admiration for Borodin, wrote a prelude
in the form of another variation on the
theme.

The "Funeral March," a brief page, is, in
the nature of things, an essay in the gro-
tesque—but utterly commonplace in other
respects.

The "Requiem" (in A minor) is a more
elaborate and more successful little miniature. After a solemn chordal passage
marked "organo," a grave "chant" theme
is announced by a "solo voice" :

Ex. 61.

Re - qui - em æ - ter - nam do - na   e - - is.

which, as will be seen, combines splendidly
with the "chopsticks" theme. This "chant"
is next given to the "chorus" in a three-part
fugal exposition; then the "organ" enters
again, and the words "et lux perpetua luceat
eis" are thundered out with full force. The
piece ends with a *fortissimo* repetition of the
introductory passage, and leaves one with a
strong impression of the ingenuity of its composer's workmanship in planning the whole
to combine with the persistent repetitions
of Ex. 60.

The posthumous "Mazurka" is even more
curious, for we recognise in its first subject
an adaptation, in $\frac{3}{8}$ time, of the principal
theme of the first mazurka of the "Petite
Suite," while the melody of the Trio is a

variation of that of the middle section of the
second mazurka from the same set of pieces.
As the $\frac{2}{4}$ time of Ex. 60 is never deviated
from, there is throughout a crossing of
rhythms which makes things rather tricky
for the non-musician who is displaying his
powers in the "primo" part!

Borodin's output as a song-writer is
scarcely larger than that for the piano, but it
is certainly more interesting and more important, and in one or two, at least, of the
songs, reaches a decidedly higher level than
any of the piano-pieces. His songs are, of
course, still miniatures, and, as we have already seen, his was not a mind which gave
of its best unless it had a large canvas on
which to paint, but, while not a born song-
writer as some men are, his productions in
this form are not, on the whole, unworthy of
his name. Borodin had not, like Moussorgsky, the art of distilling the essence of a
whole drama into the tiny compass of a short
song, but, in some respects, his best work is

by no means inferior to that of Russia's
supreme master of the art of song-writing.
Of his felicity in catching the atmosphere of
the poem which he is setting or of the accuracy of his verbal accentuation those who are
unacquainted with the Russian language
cannot, of course, judge, but if we may base
our conclusions on the English,* French and
German translations, his skill in the former
feat is generally infallible. Above all,
Borodin's genius was always pre-eminently
lyrical in its tendencies, and, despite the
fact that it seems to be slightly out of favour
with art-song composers at the present time,
true lyricism is by no means a factor to be
despised in a song. On the other hand,
while Borodin's songs are decidedly *vocal*
compositions and not piano-pieces with a

---

* Sound and workmanlike, if uninspired (as is only
natural), English translations of Borodin's songs have
been made by Mrs. Rosa Newmarch and Mr. Edward
Agate; Mrs. Newmarch has also prepared an English
version of the text of "Prince Igor."

declamatory voice-part to make them comprehensible, it must be understood that the piano-part is, in most cases, no mere background accompaniment but a definite part of the organic whole; a secondary partner in the combination, it is true, but still a real partner.   In one or two instances it is interesting to note that Borodin has adopted the now almost universal practice of building his piano-part entirely on repetitions of a single *motif* which in itself reflects in some way the general feeling of the song; only in one or two instances, however, does the accompaniment ever approach the region of actual descriptive tone-painting.

In considering Borodin's songs as a whole we find that everything of interest is included in three small sets, each of only four numbers, but wonderfully varied in scope and manner.   Of these, " The Song of the Dark Forest," the first number of the set, published by Bessel, is almost indisputably the finest song Borodin ever wrote, whether

judged from the point of view of technical
workmanship or from that of purely æsthetic
perfection; certainly it is of all the short
works the one which approaches most nearly
to the spirit of the "greater" Borodin. Its
feeling, a "tale of long ago, ages past and
gone," of primeval freedom, of the birth of
heroic nations and of bloody victory, is akin
to that of the Second Symphony, and is expressed with magnificent breadth and power.
Both voice and piano parts are entirely derived from a striking and typical theme of
savage, almost primitive grandeur:

Ex. 62.

Molto Moderato

Thro' the   for - est dark, thro' the   moan-ing trees

pesante

floats a song.

etc.

the rhythmic freedom of which is continued
to the end.   As music, pure and simple, its
massive, rough-hewn structure compels admiration; in conjunction with its fine, cutting
truth as an indictment of the degeneration
of love of liberty into lust for power it is a
perfect masterpiece, than which Moussorgsky himself wrote nothing finer.

The next song of the group, a setting of
Heine's "Aus meinen Augen" (the only instance of Borodin's using a non-Russian
text), charming as it is, is a far inferior piece
of work.*   Naturally the words demand the
lightest of treatment, and the composer has

* Comparison with Schumann's setting (in the "Dich-
terliebe") is inevitable—and not to Borodin's advantage.

provided his simple, graceful melody with
only a very slight accompaniment; an attractive little love-song which might almost
have been written by Brahms—and, indeed,
but for a few traces in the melodic line one
would have no reason to suspect the composer of non-Teutonic origin.

"The Queen of the Sea" is more elaborate and original, though decidedly inferior
to the "Song of the Dark Forest." Its atmosphere, that of the submarine fairy-king-
dom which we see in Rimsky-Korsakov's
"Sadko," is suggested throughout in the accompaniment by a continuous murmuring
quaver figure in the right-hand, to which
the sonorities of the left impart a feeling of
depth and immensity. The siren song of
the sea-maid, who seeks to entice the travel-
ler to join her in the caverns of the ocean-
bed, is not of particularly striking beauty,
but the song is successful on the whole
despite the rather hackneyed nature of its
subject; partly perhaps because the com-

poser has not yielded to the temptation of infusing any dramatic element into the lyrical nature of his conception.

The fourth song of the set, "The Wondrous Garden," is slightly akin in feeling to some of the numbers of the "Petite Suite." The voice part is almost in the nature of melodic recitative of the type we have noticed in "Prince Igor," while the accompaniment, entirely based on a drowsy, monotonous figure :

Ex. 63.
Andantino con moto

suggests the prevailing mood of the piece—a sort of amorous mysticism; an original and striking little song which does not, however, quite "come off" as one imagines the composer intended.

The set of "Four Romances," published by Jurgenson, contains Borodin's best-known, if not by any means his best, songs —"The Sleeping Princess" and "The Sea," both styled "ballads" by their composer. The very sugary charm of "The Sleeping Princess," not altogether unsuitable in treatment of the familiar sentimental tale of the sleeping beauty of the enchanted wood, is curiously French in feeling —foreshadowing quite closely the manner of Fauré, or even the earlier Debussy :*

Ex. 64.

* There is no English version of the words, and, as will be noticed, the French text (by C. Grandmousin) fits the melody abominably in its accentuation.

la   prin - cesse aux   si   doux yeux,

etc.

The piano-part, with its lulling, drowsy syncopations and figure-repetition, is typical of
Borodin's treatment of song-accompaniment
—as a background, but still a real part of
the picture, so to speak.   The title of "ballad," as also in the case of "The Sea," is
used to denote the use of a more strophic
form than usual, Borodin's shorter songs
being generally more or less "durchkom-
poniert."   In this case there are slightly
more animated episodes, dealing with the
laughter of the wood-spirits and the future
coming of a deliverer, but Ex. 64 returns
after each, and the song ends in a mood of
questioning.   Harmless, even over-sweet in

its sentimentality as we find it to-day, the
unorthodoxy of the harmony roused the ire
of at least one contemporary Russian critic*
when the song first made its appearance.
Unfortunately the titles of two of the other
songs in the same set—"Dissonance" and
"My Song is fierce and bitter"—provided ir-
resistible targets for the numerous witti-
cisms of the opposition scribes, who thus
avenged themselves for the sarcasms which
César Cui had hurled at the Rubinsteins and
their friends and for Moussorgsky's merci-
less lampooning in "The Peep-Show."
The two songs in question are, however,
fairly innocuous musically, their titles refer-
ring, of course, to sentimental "discord"
and "bitterness"—but they certainly presented heaven-set opportunities to the sar-
castically minded.

"Dissonance," the French version of its
text by the Countess Mercy Argenteau already referred to, is a brief and not unattrac-

---

* Laroche.

tive little song belonging to much the same mental and emotional world as the concluding numbers of the "Petite Suite," for piano; the accompaniment is more conventional than is usually the case with Borodin.

"My Song is Fierce and Bitter," though of no larger dimensions, is a much more important and individual utterance—striking and transfigured with tragic passion. The elasticity of the declamatory rhythms of the voice-part and the harmonic freedom of the whole were, no doubt, seized upon by Borodin's enemies as a literal fulfilment of the threat implied in the title, but the modern musician will be quite unappalled even by the consecutive fifths. An artistic touch is shown in the opening and closing of the song by the same impetuous little "capriccio" phrase on the piano which so admirably prepares and then dismisses the fugitive mood evoked by the poem.

"The Sea" (dedicated to Stassov), like "Prince Igor" and several of the other songs ("Dissonance," "The Sleeping Prin-

cess," etc.), a setting of Borodin's own words,
is a much longer and more elaborate effort
but a far less artistically-successful one; indeed one would not, perhaps, be far wrong
in considering it Borodin's worst song—
though one of the most frequently heard.
The atmosphere of the whole is too suspici-
ously akin to that of a certain once-popular
type of English ballad to be either attractive
or impressive; the sad fate of the homeward
bound sailor, his vessel laden with presents
for his lady-love, wrecked in sight of land,
has been so overdone that we need something a lot more convincing than Borodin's
rather theatrical treatment of it really to
move us very deeply. The accompaniment
almost throughout consists of tremendous
"allegro tempestuoso," piano pounding, a
frank piece of realistic tone-painting in·
tended to convey a picture of the storm, but
needless to say, an utter failure from the
emotional point of view. The only genuine
piece of artistry in the whole naïve melo-
drama is the concluding page, for piano

alone, in which the stormy semiquavers of the accompaniment gradually become quieter and finally settle down to a low murmuring, which, with the deep, hollow, sustained chords, does in a way suggest poetically the cruel, inscrutable mystery of the ocean depths.

The set of four songs published by Belaïeff, equally varied in manner and worth, seem to have been composed at a somewhat later date than the aforementioned and were, as a matter of fact, issued posthumously. The "Arabian Melody," with its Oriental passion and languor, is rendered superficially attractive by its sentimental harmonic colour (necessitated to a certain extent by the subject) but is really little more than an artistic specimen of the popular type of pseudo-orientalism familiar to all students of commercial "art" as exemplified in the modern "shop ballad."

"It was thy choice, far journey taking," while not true Borodin is on a very different level. Its type of subject, its atmosphere of

dark and heavy sentimentality, and its actual
musical treatment are similar to that of
"Dissonance," though it is built on a considerably larger scale; it is, however, tinged to a
certain extent with a feeling more German
than Russian in many respects and inevitably
suggesting comparison with Schumann, for
whom Borodin is known to have had considerable admiration and whom, indeed, he distantly resembled in many points of
temperament.

The two remaining songs, on the other
hand, are, while not resembling anything in
the bigger works, as individual as anyone
could desire; there need be no hesitation in
acknowledging both to be real masterpieces.
"Rich and Poor," with its touching musical
simplicity and its fine humanitarianism, is a
perfect gem from whatever point of view it
be judged; the pathetic dignity of the last
page, following as it does a breathless
"vivo" vision of the luxuries in which the
protagonist would indulge were he rich, is
particularly moving but the whole song is in-

stinct with real sympathy for the poor in
their heroic struggle for existence. Among
its purely musical features may be mentioned
a characteristic little phrase in the accompaniment (of which there is also an orchestral version) which opens and closes the
piece and also recurs at each pause in the
voice part. "Master Pride," as striking in
its satirical humour as "Rich and Poor" in
its pathos, recalls the type of subject which
attracted Moussorgsky in his lighter moods
and, indeed, he actually made a setting of the
same poem. Borodin's victim, a self-impor-
tant little parvenu, "three feet of nothing
when all is said," ashamed even of the hum-
ble home of his old parents, is mercilessly
ridiculed. His fussy, ostentatious strut is
suggested by the pompous "allegro moderato marciale" tramp of the accompaniment,
as well as by the vocal line, in a quite different way, but a none the less effective one
from Moussorgsky's well known sketch of a
similar character ("Samuel Goldenberg") in
the "Pictures at an Exhibition." In this

accurate analytical sketching of psychology,
" Master Pride" occupies a unique place
among Borodin's works and with it we may
fittingly conclude our survey of his minor
compositions.   Mention may, however, be
made in passing to two quite unimportant
concerted vocal pieces—a septet for voices
and piano and a humorous " Serenade of
Four Gallants to a Lady" ("Pendant que
tout dort et repose à l'entour"), for male
voice quartet, in which he was again his own
poet.   Neither are ever heard in England.

VI.—BORODIN'S POSITION IN ART.

"So far as traditional symphonic form is concerned, the master craftsman of the last quarter of the nineteenth century was not Brahms but Borodin."—Philip Heseltine.

The definite "placing" and labelling of a creative artist and his work, as if both were in the nature of interesting entomological specimens, while a pleasant, even quite fascinating amusement is of little value to anyone but the sportive critic himself. The chief purpose of a label is to provide the general artistic public with a ready made preconceived idea, instead of letting it do its thinking on its own account; yet modern musical criticism, especially, has for one of its chief objects in life the demolition of all the encrustations of pseudo-axioms which have gradually collected upon the reputations of the older masters. Hence the manufacture of fresh dogmas, some of which, however ridiculous, are sure to be at least partially accepted, is a somewhat pernicious practice which ought to be as punishable as defamation of character. Without, however, venturing to put Borodin either in a cabinet or on a pedestal there is no harm in considering the actual positive values of his work as they appear in the light of forty years of artistic progress. The value, and therefore the actual importance, of all art is of two kinds, the one bearing only partially upon the other; firstly, its direct value, its intrinsic worth as a work of beauty, and secondarily, and very little less in importance, its value as an agent in influencing the current of artistic tendencies. The work of some composers, Elgar or Dvorák, for instance, is, of course, important merely for its actual æsthetic worth, while on the other hand, that of

such men as Hector Berlioz, lives only in
that of their successors. Sometimes the seed
of an apparently isolated composer, like
Chopin, seems to have fallen upon stony
ground, only to germinate long afterwards,
as Chopin's did in Scriabin's; or, again,
critics may be led to trace a false genealogy
as in the assumption that the mantle of Field
fell upon Chopin, whereas, as a matter of
fact, it has only quite recently found a legi-
timate wearer in Arnold Bax. In Borodin's
case, however, the line of descent is sufficiently widespread and so obvious that there
is really little chance of making false deduc-
tions. Before considering this somewhat
parental aspect of the composer's importance it may be of some interest to consider
those positive qualities, so transmitted,
which enable one to affirm with perfect confidence that a great part of Borodin's work
is possessed not only of really lasting qualities, but of properties which entitle it to a
very high place indeed in musical literature.

In his own immediate circle, among his

friends of the "Kouchka," he was quite
without a rival. Cui's importance *as a composer* is practically nil and even Balakirev's
is little more. Rimsky-Korsakov's mastery
of the orchestra has tended to give his work
a somewhat fictitious value; but, however
excellent the manner, the *matter* of his music
is really quite undistinguished—while as a
technician, especially in handling large and
complicated structures, he is far inferior to
Borodin. Moussorgsky was certainly a
genius—but a very unbalanced one. His
harmonic and pictorial experiments were at
once daring, interesting and valuable,
though their unqualified success is open to
challenge, but, after all, his triumphs are all
in the non-purely musical spheres of song
and opera. As a craftsman he cannot be
considered strong, even if we admit that
much of his apparent crudity is really only
daring innovation, and as a writer of "pure"
music he is quite negligible.

Borodin alone of the "Five," has any
claims as a genuine symphonist or chamber

music composer. In these spheres even if
the success of " Prince Igor " (in a sense, his
" Fidelio ") be open to question, he undoubtedly reached great heights. In these large
scale, purely abstract works, we find the true
Borodin—the Russian tone poet and patriot
lost in contemplation of his native land,
brooding lovingly over its scenery and history, and expressing his reactions to them in
wonderful music. Nationalism is so much
the key-note of Borodin's art that one is compelled to consider its real worth as a genera-
tor of artistic expression—for it is more that
than an ideal to be sought after, as some
would have us believe. In one sense, of
course, a very broad one, practically all
genuine art derives, in some way, some sort
of influence from the creator's national environment—the Italian opulence of colour in
a Giorgione canvas, the fragile prettiness
and sparkling delicacy of a Fragonard or the
sentimental frivolity of a waltz of Johann
Strauss, each in its way is typically national.
Even music which we usually consider as

quite eclectic in feeling. Bach's organ works
or Brahms's songs for instance, is by no
means free from racial influences. At the
other extreme are those composers, like
Liszt and Grieg and Percy Grainger, whose
idea of nationalism is to take a folk-song
and treat it with all possible skill and brilliance—in other words to invest it with the
very sophistication to which folk-music is the
direct antithesis. Folk-music has, of course,
a definite place in a nationalist movement
(especially at its commencement) but merely
as an indication of the most natural ways of
expressing racial temperament in music.
The mere use, or even imitation, of folk-
song is indicative of an affection for it *per
se*, but not infrequently also of lack of individual inspiration. In any case the adoption
by a composer of a determination to be
nationalist at all costs is, in itself, a slightly
unnatural pose and tends to give an air of
insincerity to what is in its highest form, the
most sincere of artistic attitudes. It is not,
as Glinka and some of the "Kouchka" at

times thought, the letter of folk-music which matters, but the spirit; and once that spirit is absorbed into a composer's mentality it matters not a jot if he copies or does not copy its little clichés and mannerisms, which after all, as we are beginning to learn to our cost from the works of some of our own contemporary composers, tend to become more than a little wearisome with constant reiteration. Having yielded up its soul to the composer folk-song has done its part. It is in this last feat of absorption that Borodin is above all remarkable; folk-music pointed out the road for him but, except perhaps in the case of the orientally derived melodies, he is concerned with the expression of similar feelings—but not with similar expression of them, a very different thing. Of his pseudo-orientalism one feels a little more doubtful; much of it, most of it indeed, rings true enough, for even more than Rimsky-Korsakov, he had a genuinely Asiatic tinge in his mentality which as was only natural showed itself in his creations, but one feels that its truest expression is found in moods such as prevail in the Polovtsian dances and march of " Prince Igor," for instance, or the opening of the B minor Symphony. On the other hand, the slow movement of the E flat Symphony and the "Arabian Melody," for example, are too nearly akin to what has been called "Wardour Street orientalism," to be quite satisfying and, like some of Rimsky-Korsakov's less successful efforts, such as his "Antar" Symphony, too superficially " pretty" to be sincere. Of course, Rimsky-Korsakov, even in "Scheherazade," never really cuts deeper than the skin of the East; Borodin, at his best, reflects its mind just as he also reflects the mind of the Western Russian and in an even more masterly way. Again and again he shows us, not like Tchaïkovsky a *personal* soul, dark and tortured, but a *national* one in which we may read, as in the pages of Pushkin, Gogol or Tolstoy, the secrets of ·Russia's national pride, her humour and her humanitarian idealism. We may read in it, too, the terri-

ble twisted mentality of the Slavonic mind,
with, underlying its superficial western
polish, deep veins of grim horror and brooding cruelty.   The psychological aspects of
Borodin's music are therefore not merely interesting but extremely important, the more
so as the document is so curiously, startlingly
impersonal. Tchaïkovsky and Scriabin have
each given us the completest, most terrifying individual revelations, but their value in
unravelling the mysteries of Slavonic temperament is no more than that of De Quin-
cey's " Confessions," or Elgar's symphonies
and oratorios, in giving a foreigner the key
to our English mentality.   A symphony of
Elgar reveals the brain of *one* Englishman,
fired with nobility and mysticism and every
refinement and dignity of thought, it is true,
but still entirely personal; a symphony of
Vaughan Williams lays bare the secret,
innermost places of the heart and mind of
every Englishman who loves his country.
The one, as a work of art, is neither worth
more nor less than the other, but there is no

doubt that the foreigner who would seek to
learn our secret thoughts as a nation must
turn to Vaughan Williams rather than to
Elgar, though he would probably for the
very same reason find the latter more easy to
approach. So, in Russian music, it is with
Borodin and Tchaïkovsky and, again, in the
twentieth century with Stravinsky and Scriabin. Psychological value, however, has, as
we are at last beginning to learn, no very
strong life-giving properties in the realm of
art. An art-work lives, not by psychology or
philosophy or cleverness, but by its inherent
strength and beauty.

Whatever positive qualities Borodin's
music may possess it must be admitted that
actual novelty in the more meretricious
sense, is not one of them, though, indeed, it
may be questioned if novelty is really a
quality at all. It may be a help or a hind-
rance or both, to different people, to the
rapid acceptance of a work by the public or
the critics, but its real positive value is quite
nil, for the novelty of to-day is the common-

place of to-morrow and a work which has
nothing better than novelty to recommend it
becomes in a few years as dead as a herring,
a door nail or a Victorian oratorio. It must
not be supposed, however, that Borodin was
not original; he most emphatically was—but
not *consciously* so. He had individual
things to say (though not about himself) in
an individual way, but he is so anxious and
so sincere in his desire to express them, that
he can never be bothered consciously to find
new and startling channels through which to
pour them and consequently we find that,
generally speaking, mere superficial novelty
of effect is absent from his music. // Occasionally, as in the scherzo of the B minor
Symphony, for instance, he brings off some
daring and quite original *tour de force*, but
on the whole such moments are very rare
with him and he never relies, as Rimsky-
Korsakov did, in the " Capriccio Espagnol,"
for instance, on novelty alone to carry off his
music. In the case mentioned in the B minor
Symphony (a work full of entirely new

thought, yet making, on the whole, surpris-
ingly little "cheap" direct appeal) the whole
conception was new and could have been expressed in no other way, and even here the
composer makes scarcely any attempt to
please or shock us by fresh harmonic combinations, while the form is, broadly speaking, as traditional as in anything he wrote.
This absence of meretricious appeal is somewhat unique in a Russian composer, and
shows itself further in Borodin's never-failing level-headedness of expression and the
self-control of the true scientific mind which
never allowed him to indulge in the hysterical outbursts* by which artists with less
restraint are able to mesmerise an undiscern-
ing public. Some composers, such as
Sibelius, in his later phase, and Brahms,
have gone to the other extreme of reticence
by wrapping themselves to a great extent in
a cloak of grey, repellent hardness; Borodin, of course, was never of this type. His

---

* He has a literary counterpart, in this respect, in
Anton Tchekov—another medical man, incidentally.

colours, while not merely splashed about childishly for their own sake, are always entirely attractive; if the material demands the most brilliant colours of the orchestral palette they are there, if the softest, most melting delicacy of tint is required it is laid on with the most perfect certainty of touch; indeed, so much are material and colour one, that they seem in most cases to have been conceived together and at the same moment —a very different method to the vulgar laying on of instrumental colours with which such men as Tchaïkovsky have bedecked their works.   There is only one point to which exception can be taken in Borodin's methods of orchestration—the somewhat excessive use of the brass common in all Russian orchestral music; he never actually becomes merely blatant or vulgar through employing it, but it must be admitted that, to western ears, its too frequent use savours slightly of a showy cheapness which was in reality quite foreign to the composer's nature, refined and sincere.

All these matters are, however, concerned
with only the externals of music; what of the
really vital elements—melody, rhythm, harmony? As the musical quotations I have
made show fairly conclusively, Borodin was
always   attracted   to   definitely   *melodic*
themes; his lyrical nature wanted real tunes,
rather than brief, pregnant *motifs* in the
Beethoven-Brahms manner, in which to express itself. They are certainly less well
adapted to the requirements of cerebral
music and are infinitely more difficult of
development in the classical sense, but then,
as has already been stated, Borodin's
methods of "building" were not those of the
German masters. He could, as we know
from the first movement of the First Symphony, equal them at their own game, just as
he shows in the First Quartet that he is as
clever a contrapuntist as any academic
mathematician, but what he usually needed
was not a tiny *motif* as a seed from which to
grow a great organism, but an extended
melody upon which he could brood and

dwell, viewing it from a dozen angles and
subjecting it to the play of various lights
and fresh ideas, yet never treating it germin-
ally.   Other men, non-Russians like Schubert and Dvorák, have done the same and,
like Borodin, have been attacked by pedants
for a lyric fluency which to many of us is a
refreshing relief from the tortuous, cerebral
strivings of the academic mind engaged in
the solemn manipulation of themes remarkable only for their *latent* possibilities.   The
world would, however, be poorer by the loss
of Schubert's B minor Symphony than by
that of every note that Bruckner and Reger
together ever wrote or (dare one say it?) of
any one of Brahms's conscientious efforts;
surely beauty is the real criterion, not skill.
Writing of the English metaphysical poets
of the early seventeenth century, Johnson
once put the whole matter in a nutshell; they
were "men of learning," he said, "and to
show their learning was their whole endeavour, but unluckily resolving to show it in
rhyme, instead of writing poetry they only

wrote verses." We get intellectual pleasure
from Brahms, just as we do from Donne,
and both were real creators of beauty, but
that is not to say that we do not get intellectual pleasure from the music of a Borodin
or a piece of modern *vers libre*. We may
go farther and say that we actually get more
pure pleasure from a work of art in which our
mind is not too constantly distracted by the
struggles of the artist in overcoming pro-
digious technical difficulties largely of his
own making, like a German poet concocting
a sonnet. So much for the charge of "too
facile a technique" sometimes brought
against Borodin.

This ease of expression had yet another
consequence; while Moussorgsky, almost
always, and Rimsky-Korsakov, by fits and
starts and with occasional revulsions to the
strictest shackles of pedantry, burst the
bonds of traditionalism in the necessity of
finding an individual utterance, Borodin's
command of technique permitted the utmost
freedom of speech without bordering on

licence. Moussorgsky one suspects of being,
like Walt Whitman, too lazy to master technique, though, like the American, his nat·
ural, rough-hewn utterance is impressive in
its way, but Borodin, in his most purely
physical moods, never loses his characteris·
tic mental refinement; he could be daring
enough when he liked (witness the astonishing modernism of the march in "Prince
Igor"), but even then he always kept himself under control. His harmonies at times
are, indeed, as adventurous as Moussorgsky's himself, but generally speaking they
are chiefly remarkable for either massive
sonority or limpid clarity and always for
their richness of colour. Of rhythm, the
very life-blood of music, Borodin was a perfect master; in the supple elasticity of some
of his rhythms and the incisive vigour of
others he often anticipated the most modern
developments. He seldom falls into that
squareness of rhythmic invention which is
the pitfall of so many composers and the
rhythm, as well as the melodic line, of his

phrases has almost always a certain bigness of conception. His rhythms, too, are free from the mannerisms into which even a Wagner or an Elgar can fall at times. On the other hand, his melodic and harmonic thought, it must be admitted, at times tended to flow into the familiar channels which in a great composer are considered as marks of a distinctive idiom and in a little one as unfortunate mannerisms.

Borodin's inherent traditionalism in matters of form has already been alluded to, but it must never be forgotten that if not an innovator he was something far more worth while and far more difficult to become—a consummate master of musical construction on the grand scale. Mr. Philip Heseltine's sweeping assertion* which I have quoted at the beginning of this chapter is a bold one and obviously open to challenge, but any open-minded critic with an intimate knowledge of the larger works of both the

* In an article in the "Daily Telegraph," October 13, 1923.

composers thus placed in juxtaposition would
admit, at once, that there is a great deal of
truth in it.   That Brahms was, of course, a
very great composer, if with an undeservedly
great reputation in some respects, only a fool
would deny, but if we approach him with a
really unprejudiced mind we shall find that
the value of his music lies in its nobility and
its day-dreaming romantic beauty rather
than upon the qualities for which we have
been accustomed to consider it pre-eminent.
One of the hoary traditions which have long
been treasured by Brahms-worshippers is his
mastery of classic form.   Its origin is not
difficult to trace; ever since Beethoven's
death there had been a gradual slump in
classic ideas and more especially in the use
of classic forms.   Beethoven himself had in
his later works started the search for new
methods of structural design and, in the
hands of the more conservative Romantics
like Chopin, Schumann and Mendelssohn,
the traditional forms seemed to be gradually
petering out and losing their vitality, till in

the latter half of the last century the only practitioner in this direct line of descent (in both senses of the word) was Anton Bruckner, whom we rightly regard in England as of comparatively little importance.

Coevally a new idea, also deriving much of its inspiration from Beethoven, was gaining strength and influence—that of programme-music, developing through the progressive Romantics, Berlioz and Liszt, till it found its proper sphere and its highest development (not in the concert-hall, at all) in the music-dramas of Wagner. This new doctrine, that symphonic music should take its form from exterior foreign influences in · stead of being naturally conditioned by purely abstract musical ideas, was, of course, repellent to many sound musicians who were acute enough to see that the programmists had only found a blind-alley instead of a new road, and that the symphonic poem, tied hand and foot to its literary basis, was, in reality, far less " free " than the classic symphony, unfettered by any considerations ex-

cept those of artistic balance.   In these good
people Johannes Brahms found a willing
audience; here, said they, was a man who
could compose music capable of standing on
its *own* legs, music, moreover, which was un-
deniably of better quality than anything
(Wagner, of course, was in the other camp
and therefore beyond the pale) since Beethoven; here was a man who was proving that
there was still life in the traditional forms
and, not only that, but that they were capable of further elaboration and development; there was apparently no one else living who could do anything like as much—
therefore, and it was here they went wrong,
Brahms was the supreme master of form and
a model for all good young students for al!
time.   He had no rivals in Germany, but
only because (except for Wagner, who was
not writing music *as* music but only as an
element of music-drama) Germany was suf-
fering from a slump in composers. England
was still enjoying the second-hand Mendels-
sohnisms of Sterndale-Bennett and others;

Italy had only an operatic composer, Verdi;
in France there was a similar lacuna, though
César Franck was plodding his quiet way,
ignored by the world; only in Russia was
there any live music-making which attracted
the world's notice, and, unfortunately, Russia was for too long supposed to be repre-
sented by the vapid commonplaces of Anton
Rubinstein and the intoxicating but obviously programmatic and unbalanced works
of Tchaïkovsky; Cui, Balakirev and Moussorgsky left abstract symphonic music
severely alone, and nobody could seriously
consider Rimsky-Korsakov as a rival to
Brahms.   Borodin had certainly written two
symphonies and two string quartets, amongst
other things, which compelled admiration—
but the bare idea of comparing a Russian
amateur with a German *professional* never
occurred to anybody, it was altogether too
absurd.   That it was not so, we know now.
In speaking of Borodin's methods of thematic treatment, reference was made to the
superiority of his ease and fluency over the

laboured efforts of the academics with their too obvious show of erudition; the same thing applies to his structural conceptions. As a framework for his thoughts, however original the latter might be, the traditional forms, with the usual slight modifications made by every composer, were perfect and as he used them with consummate ease and total absence of conscious effort the result is, in the B minor Symphony, structural perfection. Brahms, on the other hand, always seems to be engaged in a battle with his ideas in order to fit them into his previously conceived model; this alone causes a feeling of stiffness, with his innovations in the elaboration of bridge-passages, etc., it produces a blurring of outlines and a general feeling of clumsiness and effort, heightened by the composer's too laborious working out of the possibilities of his themes. " Nur wenn Dir die Form ganz Klar ist wird Dir der Geist klar werden," said another German,* and in

---

* Schumann.

Brahms we often find that the spirit of the music is smothered by the way in which it is expressed. This is never the case with Borodin, the soul of whose art is directness of expression and who furthermore knew, as Brahms so often did not, when he had exhausted his topic. The fact that his topics were usually more alive than those of the German composer has already been alluded to. Without labouring the point further or setting up a sort of posthumous rivalry between two entirely different composers which never existed in reality, it may be confidently assumed that Mr. Heseltine's observation is based on quite sound, common-sense reasoning.

In one thing, and one thing only, Borodin was lacking to possess every quality of the greatest composers—universality of emotional range. He touched upon many varieties of feeling with great success, but in others, important ones, he was singularly less skilful; his musical sense of humour was but slight, mystery or anything approaching it was foreign to his straightforward, open nature, human love he was generally rather unsuccessful in depicting; still more remarkable is the entire absence of expression of any kind of religious feeling* in his music. These are shortcomings, deficiencies that each must account for in his own way, but we may well be satisfied with a man who has given us so much wealth and not grumble that he has not given us more.

The power of genius has, moreover, to be measured not only by its immediate creative results but by the extent to which it is a generating force in its influence on other minds. The influence of the " Invincible Band," as a body, though very important, took strangely different channels from what might have been expected. On the general course of the development of modern European music their ideas have left the most marked

---

* Except a sort of pagan nature-worship.

traces.   Everyone knows how Debussy, and
hence the entire Impressionist school of
music, was enormously affected by Moussorgsky, himself an entire realist, especially
in his opening up of new harmonic paths,
and the revelation of new, undreamed of
worlds of brilliant orchestral colour brought
about something like a revolution in the post-
Wagnerian world of music, especially in
France.   Still more important was the im-
petus given to nationalist ideals and the use
of folk-song, so much needed in the England of that time, stifled with German ideas
and methods.   Our own nationalist school
of the present day may not have much in
common with the beliefs of the " Band," but
it nevertheless has derived, directly and in-
directly, to a surprising extent from it.   In
Russia itself, however, where one would
naturally have expected its influence to have
been most evident it failed to bear any very
valuable fruit and gradually fizzled out, with
such men as Liadov, Glazounov and Lia-
pounov, into a mere dull respectability which

might pardonably be mistaken for the products of the school of the Rubinsteins and Tchaïkovsky.

It was not, indeed, until about 1909 that any composer appeared as a worthy successor to the members of the " Kouchka " and working on the lines they had laid down. In that year appeared Igor Stravinsky's ballet-opera, " Le Rossignol," a work which, in conjunction with its successor, the better-known " L'Oiseau de Feu," stamped its composer as the true heir to the " Kouchka." With an extraordinarily individual mentality of his own Stravinsky combines the daring of a Moussorgsky and the orchestral mastery of a Rimsky-Korsakov (whose pupil he actually was), but of all the Five the one to whom he undoubtedly owes most is Borodin, who died only five years after Stravinsky's birth. His mentality, strongly Oriental in its type, is essentially very similar to that of Borodin and in its expression, even superficially, he has many interesting points of resemblance.

Even such an early work of Borodin's as
the First Symphony has left its mark on
Stravinsky, as may be seen by comparing
Ex. 2 with the opening bars of the "Ronde
des Princesses" in "L'Oiseau de Feu," for
instance, while there can be no doubt that
the Polovtsian march and dances, and other
of the most characteristic pages of "Prince
Igor" have left distinct traces on the mind
of the younger man in the riotous splendour
of the "Danse Infernale" and final tableau
of "L'Oiseau de Feu" and in many passages of "Petrouchka." Even his melodic
lines, often very beautiful in his earlier
works, are often Borodinesque in contour,
and in the bassoon solo which opens "Le
Sacre du Printemps" we can trace the genealogy directly from such melodies as Exs.
19, 23 and 52, not so much in mannerisms
like the little appoggiatura *motifs* as in the
state of mind which inspired them. "Le
Sacre du Printemps," probably the first
really mature production of the composer,
yet still regarded by most as the limit be-

yond which they cannot follow him, is indeed full of Borodin's spirit, or, rather, of one phase of it. The similarity of its general outlook with that of the first movement of the B minor Symphony has already been remarked upon, and it is instructive to notice, too, that the attitude of so many critics toward the one work was only a reflection of that of their colleagues of forty years ago toward the other. There is even a sort of monotony in the unvaried terms of the abuse; "anarchy," "nihilism"—the same old cat-calls that were probably hurled at Monteverde, or would have been if nihilism had been invented in his time. Yet, as we have seen, Borodin, far from being a musical Bolshevist, was really the profoundest respecter of tradition, and his B minor Symphony is to-day everywhere regarded as an intellectual masterpiece of the first rank. There is this difference however with Stravinsky, that he lacks the orderliness of Borodin's scientific mind, and, whereas, in this very symphony and in some of the

"Prince Igor" dances in the same mood, the latter never becomes incoherent even in the expression of the most primitive and elemental human passions, the most naked savagery and ferocious exuberance, Stravinsky is very frequently unable to control his self-expression. Hence his large-scale works, hampered by the requirements of choregraphic scenarios, which, whatever he may say to the contrary, cannot permit of thought in purely musical terms, are structurally almost boneless, so to speak. Yet this faculty of orderliness, control, selection, call it what you will, is often all that distinguishes the ravings of a lunatic from the outpourings of a genius. Nobody would be foolish enough now seriously to consider Stravinsky a lunatic, but there is no doubt Stravinsky a lunatic, but there is no doubt that this failure to control an over-heated imagination* and to prune and train its products is a serious defect in an artistic mentality.

---

* Cf. the ridiculous extravagancies of Strauss, at times, and the freakishness which spoils some of Beethoven's finest work.

Borodin never had this, and, whereas by far the greater proportion of Russian art and literature is as mentally unbalanced as Stravinsky's music in this respect, one's prevailing feeling as to the older man is a strong conviction of his unfailing fundamental sanity.   He is, for all that, more accurate in his expression of the Russian mind and soul than any of the excitable neurotics, and while their paroxysms are merely repellent to the sober Western mind, we are able to enjoy Borodin even when he is depicting the most frightful traits of national character. To wield this power, as well as to create the most pure, unsullied beauty, is only the gift of a very great artist, and as such we must consider Alexander Borodin—the supreme justification of the amateur in music.

ML410
.B73A4
1976

Abraham

Borodin